Celebration!

Celebration!

Ten Principles of More Joyous Living

JAROLDEEN ASPLUND EDWARDS

Deseret Book Company
Salt Lake City, Utah

Library of Congress Cataloging-in-Publication Data

Edwards, Jaroldeen Asplund.
    Celebration! : ten principles of more joyous living / Jaroldeen Asplund Edwards.
        p.   cm.
    Includes bibliographical references and index.
    ISBN 1-57345-021-9
    1. Christian life—Mormon authors. 2. Time management—Religious aspects—Church of Jesus Christ of Latter-day Saints. 3. Women—Time management. 4. Joy—Religious aspects—Church of Jesus Christ of Latter-day Saints. I. Title.
BX8656.E416   1995
248.4'89332—dc20   95-21417
                                                                    CIP

Printed in the United States of America

10   9   8   7   6   5   4   3   2   1

Contents

Are you sitting comfortably? Then I'll begin.

Julia S. Lang, 1921–

There is no duty we so much underrate as the duty
of being happy.

Robert Louis Stevenson 1850–1894

....

A Basketful of Thoughts
on Celebration

*O*ne bright summer morning as I was walking down the main street of Laguna Beach, a man fell
into step beside me. I glanced over, slightly alarmed,
and saw that it was one of the several homeless men
who make the beach their summer refuge.

He was dressed in discarded clothing: an old army
coat tied with a rope, filthy trousers, strips of discol-
ored rags wound around his feet and legs, and an
ancient, broken backpack over one shoulder. His hair
was grizzled, long and wild, and his beard, the same
gray as his hair, was an untamed bush that reached
down to his chest.

His face was baked by the sun to the color of
mahogany, deeply wrinkled from long exposure to the
elements and creased with dirt, but his eyes were an
astonishingly clear blue. Despite all his layers of dirt
and neglect, there was something dignified about him.
In his erect bearing and his lean, craggy face, I felt the

1

essence of the true man behind the tragic facade, and my uneasiness abated.

The street was busy, and because I walk with a slight limp (the result of an automobile accident), I thought I would look ridiculous trying to outwalk the man, so I relaxed and simply kept my pace. He walked in step beside me as though we were old friends. He was muttering to himself, and since it seemed I was destined to keep him company, I decided to listen to what he was saying. When he observed that I was listening, he directed his words toward me.

"It's like I say," he declared cheerily. "I don't know why I bother to get up in the morning. Feet don't work. Legs don't work. Eyes don't work. Stomach don't work." A pause. "Head don't work too good neither."

Something about the way he said the last sentence made me smile involuntarily. He saw my smile and exclaimed, "It's the absolute truth, ma'am. Head don't work. Matter of fact—I'm just plumb crazy!" He said this in a voice of such great good cheer that I laughed out loud. I couldn't help it. I stopped walking and turned to look at him. He stopped walking, too, but continued talking. "Yup. Like I say, nothing works. So I ask you—what else is there to do on a beautiful morning like this but get up, look at the sky, laugh, and be happy!" He broke into a gap-toothed smile, and as we grinned at one another, he began to laugh.

It was a wonderful, irresistible laugh, gentle and rueful, as though he had taken all the misery of his life and faced it, accepted it, and learned to appreciate both life's absurdity and its joy. His good humor was so infectious that I laughed, too.

There we stood on the street corner, laughing

together into the sun: two friends who might never meet again. In the midst of our difficult and imperfect lives, we had shared a brief moment of pure, wonderful, human celebration.

Celebration is the conscious decision to live our lives with joy. In the midst of turmoil, pain, and adversity, in bad times and good, joy is the great companion our Heavenly Father intended us to have. To feel joy, however, requires a decision on our part—a chosen approach to life, a chosen attitude, a constant awareness. This decision is the necessary beginning to recognizing, feeling, and developing the joy with which Heavenly Father has filled our creation.

To live with celebration we must begin with an absolute and personal conviction that we have the ability to change our lives in small, meaningful ways. We must feel that we can learn better patterns of thinking, feeling, and doing that will allow us—wherever we are individually at this moment—to feel better, accomplish more, and rise higher.

The ability to live with celebration centers on three things: first, faith in the Lord's great plan for mortal happiness; second, the determination to examine our own lives to know what will truly bring us joy; and third, the acquiring of skills and knowledge with which to create joy. We do not necessarily have to do more but rather do differently the things we are already doing—to live with a retrained point of view.

Anyone can live with a sense of celebration: working women, busy mothers, single women, older women, teenagers—everyone.

Celebration is self-made. Very slight changes in our attitudes, in the way we use our time, and in our knowledge of ourselves and of the Lord can bring enormous rewards.

Our Father in Heaven will not force our hearts to feel positive emotions. He wants us to use our God-given agency to choose happiness, to create our own celebrations and measures of joy. The Lord gives us all the raw materials, but he leaves it to us to learn how to find joy in what he has given.

The experience of trying to develop a new understanding, of looking with new vision at familiar things, reminds me of an incident in the movie *The Scarlet Pimpernel*. Percy, the dashing Scarlet Pimpernel who rides off periodically to rescue endangered nobility during the French Revolution, lives in disguise as a carefree dandy. Everyone in the audience knows instantly that he is not the fop he pretends to be, but his wife has never penetrated his disguise.

In one of my favorite scenes, the Pimpernel's wife sees Percy leaving unexpectedly. (Of course, he has done this umpteen times before.) She has lived with him for years and frequently watched him gallop away at a moment's notice with his band of debonair young men. She has noticed the dramatic change in his manner and dress and has recognized that his absences coincide with the exploits of the Pimpernel in France, and yet, until this moment when she is left alone in her husband's study (a room she has visited many times before), none of those obvious clues has given her the slightest suspicion of who he really is. As she glances about the room, her eye falls upon the moldings at the ceiling, and for the first time in all her years of marriage she notices that the pattern of the molding is a carved pimpernel (a small, distinctive flower). Her eyes open in startled recognition, and then she begins to really look at the familiar room as though she were seeing it for the first time. She stares at the fireplace—sure enough, more pimpernels carved across the mantel and on the supports. She looks at his desk—yes, more pimpernels.

For years she has sat in this room surrounded by pimpernels, but this is the first time she has really looked at them. Suddenly, now that she has noticed them, the room is a garden of pimpernels. Finally, she looks up at the life-sized portrait of her husband above the mantel. There, on his finger, is the family crest on the ring he has been wearing the whole time. And the crest? A scarlet pimpernel.

The point is, we can be walking through a world of scarlet pimpernels, but until we start looking with scarlet-pimpernel eyes, we might not see them.

Celebration—which I define as the conscious creation of happiness and joy in our own lives—is built on the patterns, emotions, and events that attend a heightened awareness of what joy is and of what our responsibilities for our own happiness are. A life of celebration will be the natural flower of the principles of faith, gratitude, knowledge, and obedience.

We misunderstand the nature of joy if we think that it is something that "happens" to us—an emotion that is inserted into our hearts or a bonus offered from outside. The admonition to feel joy is given not as a reward but as a commandment. By implication we realize that if we are commanded to be joyful—of good cheer, filled with gladness—those feelings must be within the scope of our own abilities and require our own decisions and efforts.

The source of all joy is the Lord. He has filled this earth and our lives with all the possibilities for joy. As

Luke describes it, in "good measure, pressed down, shaken together, and running over" is the way the Lord gives (Luke 6:38). But to feel joy in our hearts, to experience it in our daily lives, and to live with it through adversity and prosperity, we must teach and train our hearts and our minds. We must learn to focus on our gifts, blessings, and potential rather than on our hurts and trials. We have to believe that living joyfully is within our power and that the Lord expects us to do so today—not "when our ship comes in."

We have heard many stories of people who have spent their lives in grim and silent suffering as they worked toward a single goal that they believed would give them joy. One such story tells of a young couple who wanted a beautiful home. They were certain that when they owned a home that was as large and elaborate as those of their neighbors, their lives would be filled with joy. Until then, life would just be hard work. The couple scrimped and saved, denying themselves and their children all the simple pleasures. They worked through Saturdays and holidays, neglecting all the sweet and tender years of their children's growing up. They had no birthday parties, few presents, no family outings or vacations. Life was hard and cheerless, but how, they asked themselves, could anyone expect to be happy in their tiny, cramped, old house? They needed their dream house to be happy.

Everything bright and light-hearted disappeared in the grim feeling that the only purpose of each day was to labor for the imagined future. Kind words, patience, treats, fun, humor, and freedom—all were put aside for some later date when the family would live in the impressive home where joy would be waiting.

The grayness of their daily lives was alleviated only

by the thought of that dreamed-of house. And so the parents pinched and struggled their way toward joy.

After twenty-five years the couple finally built the lovely home they had spent their lives working toward. It was everything they had ever dreamed of, with its ample bedrooms and splendid furnishings. They moved in, expecting joy to be waiting there for them. But the rooms of the mansion were empty of joy. The children had long since grown and scattered, their childhood memories dull and cheerless. Now, busy with their own lives, they had little desire to come home to visit.

Indeed, the rooms of the great new house were empty of all the things that had been neglected through the years. The mansion was empty of laughter, family, friends, warmth, and fun because the parents had failed to feel or create those things. The parents discovered in their huge, hollow home one of the great truths about joy: a family that cannot be happy in a cottage cannot be happy in a mansion. Happiness is not a place—it is a way of life.

Joy is not found in the waiting rooms of our dreamed-of tomorrows. True joy must be found in the crowded, complex, painful, challenging, cluttered rooms of "right now." We should ask ourselves honestly how many of us are living our lives in just the same way as those unwise people. We may not be waiting for a bigger house, perhaps, but are we always waiting for someone or something to make us feel joy? Are we expecting to find happiness waiting for us when we have crossed some barrier or hurdle?

Joy is not a reward for which we must wait until our distant, celestial life. The Lord's plan is a plan of happiness; clearly, he does not intend happiness to be inaccessible. He wants us to be joyful now, in the midst of mortal stress, adversity, and sorrow. We are that we might have joy and have it more abundantly—and have it now. Isn't that good news?

Perhaps we are waiting for the Lord to show us the way to joy, but the truth is, he has already given us the example and the means. He loves us very much, and like a tender father who sends his child away to school, he wants us to be happy here. He yearns for us to live the great plan of happiness by using his blessings and following his example as we gather our own baskets of joy.

Our grandson Randall, just barely two years old, was visiting from New York. One evening he was up past his usual bedtime, and he had entered that frenzy of activity typical of an overtired toddler. He emptied the toy box, the bookshelf, and the family room drawers, but nothing interested him. He was wandering frantically looking for something to do, something to engage his attention. He had explored the rooms so often that there was nothing to satisfy him. He walked toward his mother, who was in the kitchen fixing him some warm milk, and for the first time he noticed the two cupboard doors under the stove top counter. He had thought he knew our house inside out, but suddenly, here was something new and unexpected.

In an instant he had dashed over and flung open the doors of my pots and pans cupboard. He was so astonished by what he saw that he literally took a step backward and stared in open-mouthed amazement.

"Wow!" he whispered to himself, his eyes as big as saucers, "Look at all this stuff!"

Pots and pans enough to delight the most avid

two-year-old—and they had been there all the time. How had he missed it? He was ecstatic.

When we start looking for the Lord's patterns of celebration they are all, like my pots and pans, right there, almost under our noses—all around us. Beauty, joy, and glory everywhere! They are there all the time and yet are so little observed. Cupboardfuls of wonderful things! If we open the right doors, we too will be amazed. "Wow, look at all this stuff!"

If we read the scriptures carefully, we can discover the Lord's own patterns and principles of conscious, consistent celebration. The Lord celebrates the earth itself. He celebrates and rejoices in relationships, human events, family, worship, teaching, work—everything. By discovering the Lord's principles of creating celebration and joy, we can learn how to practice those same principles.

When we search the scriptures for examples of the Lord's designs of happiness in his life and in his dealings with his children, we begin to discern his principles of living with celebratory joy. When we look, we see examples of the Lord's principles of celebration in the most familiar and unexpected passages of scripture.

What was the Garden of Eden, if not the most splendid celebration of beauty, growth, and creativity ever imagined? The Lord himself says that he placed in the garden every tree that was pleasing to the eye and to the taste—every lovely thing. It pleased him.

He created a profusion of lovely things as a celebration of creation. He didn't have to make such a variety—raspberries, strawberries, blackberries, blueberries, currants, thimbleberries, and all the other delicious and delightful gifts—the work itself, done beautifully, was his way of celebrating.

He intended that his children should celebrate, too. To Adam he said, "Go forth, dress this earth and have joy therein" (see Abr. 5:11). In other words, adorn the earth—make it more beautiful. Celebrate, as did the Lord, with work and creativity.

Another principle of joy was shown when the Lord finished each day's creation. He paused and regarded his handiwork with profound savor and celestial delight. He saw that it was good! He assessed his work and celebrated it with words and feeling. And when he finished the whole of the earth, he took a day off for rest and joy.

How often do we pause to celebrate the important moments? Often we just move on to the next duty. But the principle of living with joy and celebration taught by our Lord's example is that we should pause in our labors and take time to rest and rejoice.

In many ways, the completion of the Garden of Eden was the most splendid birthday party ever given, celebrating the birthday of mankind. Think how the garden must have looked—birds festooning the air, the munificence of sun and rain, the glories of the clear, new skies. What great party decorations!

How can we fail to see in all these things a parallel for the way in which we should celebrate, treasure, and adorn this earth, our homes, and our own lives?

The Lord has shown us how to use creativity, love, and wisdom to transform a necessary task into a celebration. The story of Noah and the ark is a good example. The Lord could have just lifted Noah's family and the animals above the water, as he lifted up the city of Enoch, and then returned them after the Flood.

Instead, he used Noah's talents and efforts, showed Noah how to build the ark, and helped him bring the magnificent beasts aboard.

The scriptures tell us that the Lord smiled on the ark and carried it in his hand. Celebration!

As I read Noah's story in the scriptures, I envision all the children through the centuries who have had toy arks with tiny animals, two by two, holding them in their hands and smiling just as the Lord did. What a splendid toy the ark makes! What a lasting celebration of the Lord's love, of the wonders of this earth, and of the great adventure of the mighty flood.

When the adventure was over, the Lord celebrated the end of Noah's journey with one of the most magnificent symbols ever designed: the rainbow arching across the clearing skies, trailing every splendid color of the spectrum over a newly washed world! That visual expression of God's covenant with man is a tremendous example of how the Lord takes an essential task and creates in it a celebration of wonder and delight.

I wonder if, at the moment of disembarking, Noah's wife was worrying about how she was going to clean up all the mud. I believe the spectacle of the rainbow would have made the mud seem unimportant. That is the miracle of what a heart of celebration can do—it can change our focus from the drudgery of life to the sublimity.

Another example of the Lord's design of living with celebration is seen in how frequently the Lord takes his prophets to the summit of mountains to teach and confer with them. Instead of a dull meeting, he creates a celebration in the high and glorious places of the earth, giving both spiritual and physical renewal.

In the accumulation of varied scriptural examples, as we observe and analyze them, we see the Lord's principles of celebration emerging. These are patterns we should emulate. After Adam was sent from the Garden of Eden, he learned firsthand the challenges and adversity of mortality. Nonetheless, Adam, rejoicing, "blessed God . . . , saying: . . . in this life I shall have joy. . . . Eve, his wife, heard all these things and was glad" (Moses 5:10–11).

One of my daughters has a favorite saying: "Duty makes us do things well; love makes us do them beautifully." If those words describe the measure of love, then we are surrounded with inexhaustible evidence of how much our Heavenly Father loves us, for he has made our world beautiful. He wants us to create our own lives with love—beautifully, not with gray drudgery. That is the pattern the Lord has set.

Every single day upon this mortal earth begins and ends with heavenly fireworks—the rising and setting of the sun, the first and last great celebrations of each mortal day. I have stood on the endless plains of Canada, on frozen lakes in upstate New York, in burning deserts, on tall mountains, on the hills of Galilee, and everywhere, everywhere, as the sun rises and sets, I have looked at the glorious festival of the sky, the splendid celebration of the Lord's creation, and the reassurance that this beautiful earth turns on its axis in the orbit for which it was designed—not just with steadfast, plodding duty but with a blaze of splendor that promises tomorrow will as surely and truly come as it will surely and truly go.

With the fireworks of sunrise and sunset, the Lord celebrates each ordinary day of our life. Should not we do the same? To celebrate our daily lives we should make the splendor of the earth a part of it. Develop patterns of personal delights. Bask in moments of quiet, music, hiking, letter-writing, woodworking, sewing, cooking, traveling, talking, serving, working, reading, loving. In the cluttered crevasses of our daily lives, create our own fireworks of joy.

I do not pretend it is a simple thing to live a life in which we create celebration. We must wrest happiness from the daily, hard stuff of our challenging and sometimes disappointing lives. We must build it into the repetitive, painful, and discouraging moments.

It can be done—in small increments, with slight and creative changes. Not big changes, just wise ones. It isn't a prescribed program or a flight of stairs that must be climbed—it is tiny changes of feelings and methods, knowledge and attitudes, and the will to be and feel in better ways. It is done at our own pace, in our own way. There is no timetable or how-to book, only the learning of new principles on which to design ways to reinforce positive feelings and experiences.

The best thing about celebration is that it builds on itself. It is both the start and the finish, the means and the end to joy. That is why it is so important for us to learn the skills that make celebration possible.

A young couple were married shortly after the young man's mission. He and his wife were students and working very hard. On a Wednesday afternoon the young husband realized they had no obligations the coming Saturday and eagerly proposed to his wife that they go on their first camping trip together. She was as elated at the idea as he was.

They both worked hard through the week, finishing classes, getting assignments and jobs completed, and, late on Friday, after a hurried bite of supper, they put their camping gear in their old car and drove about four hours to a remote spot in southern Utah. They arrived in the dark, threw up their small tent, pulled out their sleeping bags, and fell into heavy slumber.

The next morning, the young man was the first to waken. He opened the flap of the tent and walked out into the early morning sunshine with eager anticipation. Before him stretched an empty landscape and his car. Nothing was going on.

"I had the funniest feeling," he told us afterward. "Always when I had gone camping it had been as a boy, with the family. I was used to finding that the minute I got out of the tent, the fun began! But here I was, on a camping trip, awake, and outside the tent. I stood there waiting for the fun—and nothing happened!"

He ducked back into the tent and spoke to his wife. "What shall I start fixing for breakfast?" She woke and looked at him in confusion. "I don't care," she murmured. "Whatever you brought."

In an instant it became clear that each of them thought the other had arranged the food and activities. They took inventory. No matches. No food. No wood. No water. No canteens. No clean clothes. No map of the area—no planning—no fun.

As he told the story, the young man laughed at himself. "All my life the fun was just there, waiting for me. I didn't fully realize until that moment that someone had to create the means by which the fun was generated. I thought fun was something automatic. You just had to go to the right place, and there it was."

At that moment, he explained, "I found out that fun is the result of somebody's efforts—it has to be made.

It also dawned on me that now it was my turn to be the one to make it—for myself and for others."

The happy part of this story is that, like the young man, we can all learn how to create celebration. When we walk out of the tents that shelter us from the night, we won't be expecting joy to be waiting for us, created by someone else. We will gradually have learned how to bring delight with us, how to build it within us, how to create it wherever we are.

Creating joy is the full purpose of celebration. It is ultimately the finest, most godlike way to live. It is City of Enoch living—and it is very contagious. When we live by the Lord's grand design of happiness, not only are our own lives blessed but the lives of everyone within our circle of influence are blessed as well.

The development of celebration in our lives is a joyful task. It has no taskmaster—only love—and its only purpose is to increase happiness. It is accomplished in just one small, self-chosen step at a time. Even in the fullest life, there is time to cultivate more joyful patterns of living. Goethe said, "One always has time enough, if one will apply it well."

There are many ways to celebrate. We are, happily, the architects of the style and manner in which we rejoice in our own circumstances, talents, satisfactions, perceptions, family, goals, and delights. As one of my sons said, "An orange probably tastes different to everyone who tastes it. But it still tastes good to all of them."

There is no one way to celebrate and no step-by-step pattern for joy. Happiness is a highly individual and personal experience that will come forth from our own unique needs and feelings and from our own talents and perceptions. The important thing is that we are striving to feel and create it and searching for principles that will help us understand how.

This personal interpretation of principles is illustrated by a story told by a sister in our ward. This wonderful woman and her husband had helped bring a family from Vietnam to the United States. On the night the Vietnamese family arrived in America, my friend, in joy and celebration, had prepared an American feast for the Vietnamese family. She had prepared roast beef, mashed potatoes, apple pie, and cinnamon rolls. She wanted the new family to celebrate in their new country.

The Vietnamese family, used to a diet of rice, vegetables, and chicken, could not eat even a bite. Though they tried to be polite, the unfamiliar food, which to us would have been a joyous feast, was to them a nightmare.

The principle of feasting in celebration is a principle that is taught and lived by the Lord himself. The principle of feasting is the same for all humankind—but when we celebrate around the world, our tables are spread to individual tastes, delights, and wonders. That is one of the joys of celebration. We get to choose our own interpretation of true principles of joy.

My favorite expression of the Lord's exhortation to live with joy is found in the words of a glorious hymn:

> *Rejoice, the Lord is King!*
> *Your Lord and King adore!*
> *Mortals, give thanks, and sing*
> *And triumph evermore.*
>
> *Lift up your heart!*
> *Lift up your voice!*
> *Rejoice, again I say, rejoice!*
> (*Hymns of The Church of Jesus Christ of*
> *Latter-day Saints*, 1985, no. 66)

I like that hymn enormously—it tells us how we should be. When I am ninety-plus years old, I hope that I, like the aged Miriam the prophetess, standing on the very edge of the endless wilderness, will feel such impelling gladness that I will pick up the timbrel, streaming with bright, rainbow-colored ribbons, and lead my friends and sisters in a great dance of celebration, singing, as did she, in praise of the Lord. A lifetime—a habit—of celebration.

"Where shall I begin, please your majesty?"
he asked. "Begin at the beginning,"
the King said, gravely,
"and go on till you come
to the end; then stop."

Lewis Carroll (Charles Lutwidge Dodgson), 1832–1898

1

....

By and Large, the Dishes Come First

*W*ork is much more fun than fun," declared Noel Coward in a moment of enthusiasm. Of course, we know that is not always true—but it is true that fun itself is more fun when our work is under control. So, although it may seem odd to start out talking about celebration by talking about work, it is necessary to do so. Work—basic order—is the foundation of all celebration.

Don't you just love the parable of the woman looking for her lost piece of silver? (see Luke 15:8–9). She lights a candle so that every corner of her house is in view. My natural temptation would be to let the light remain dim as I began the task of cleaning my whole house. I would rather not face all the corners and edges I have neglected. But the point of the parable is that the woman is seeking something of value, something she has lost and is determined to find. The manner in which she works is important, and she is determined and hopeful that she will succeed.

So the woman lights the room. Now she can see the hidden dust, the cobwebs, the stacks of things to be sorted and put away, and she begins to clean. She sweeps diligently and accepts the responsibility of the work on her own. I envision her like Snow White dusting, washing, and cleaning the cottage of the Seven Dwarfs, replacing the film of dust with shining surfaces and sweet fragrance.

At last her labors are rewarded: she finds what she is looking for, and in the process her house has been cleaned and made perfect.

In the parable, she finishes her work, and then comes the celebration. Immediately. The celebration is as much a part of the labor—and of the success—as the work itself. She calls in her neighbors and friends, and they rejoice together.

Simply put, she gives a huge party. But the party was purchased by her labors. Her celebration is not just about the recovered piece of silver but about the whole process of living—work, home, family, friends, the bounties of the earth, and the achievement of a goal. Celebrating the event gave purpose, meaning, and lasting value to her work.

This parable is a profound illustration of the way we should view both our labors and our joys.

The party the woman gave was probably more fun than the housework (I'm not saying more satisfying, just more fun), and the celebration gave value and joy to the great effort of searching, cleaning, and finding.

Basic order is essential for us to experience joy to create celebrations and happiness in our lives to the fullest extent.

Work accomplished gives us feelings of personal worth and self-esteem. When we finish tasks, we feel capable and valued—empowered. We feel renewed confidence when we are able to achieve orderliness in our environment and responsibilities. With our labors under control, we are relieved of feelings of guilt or unworthiness when we make time for play and celebration.

Peace of mind is an important ingredient of happiness. (Notice I said when our work is "under control," not when it is "done." Work is never finished. Individual jobs may be completed, but the dimension of work itself is a moving boundary that we never reach.)

We should use work undone not as a rod of guilt but as a challenge. We need to believe in ourselves, believe that we are smarter than the work, more capable than the challenge, stronger and more important than any task. Then we can delight in work done, and fix our eyes on our accomplishments more than on our failings.

It is important to recognize the unending nature of work. Many people believe they will be able to rejoice only when the work is "done." The Lord does not expect that. Work is an eternal part of the process of living, even for the Lord. In Moses 1:39 we read that we are the Lord's work and his glory, and in that familiar scripture is verified the fact that glory and work go hand in hand and are eternal. So we seek orderliness and control of our work, not the end of labor.

Another way in which work is the foundation of celebration is that it provides the means by which we create celebratory events and activities. It provides the financial means, and it also supplies the planning and preparations necessary for successful happy times.

Celebration means more to us when it is bought

with anticipation, planning, effort, and sacrifice. Great celebration can only be created with great effort—just like the earth itself. The tumult of creation was followed by the sweet celebration of the heavens and the Lord's joy: "It is good." Anticipation as we labor to prepare is part of every wonderful celebration, and it intensifies our joy.

When tasks are finished or laid aside in an orderly way, there is such a glorious sense of relief and satisfaction that the moment itself becomes a celebration.

One of the best moments of a party is the pause before the guests arrive and you look at your house, shining and clean from your labors, the food on the buffet, the lights and candles, the flowers, the hush of anticipation waiting for joyous friends and the creation of new memories. The glow of work well done—the quiet, inward celebration before the celebration.

Celebration needs the contrast of work, just as all other things need their opposites. Our family had an experience that vividly illustrates that principle.

Several years ago we were invited, along with several thousand others, to the opening of the first Great America amusement park. What an incredible experience! As we stood with our twelve children waiting to be admitted to the park, our twelve-year-old son said, "I can't wait for the gates to open, Mother. I think when those gates open, it will be the best thing that has ever happened in this world."

You see, for that one night, it was going to be just like Pleasure Island in *Pinocchio*. Everything was to be free.

My son and his cousin, who was the same age, begged to be allowed to go at their own pace, wherever they wished. Because the amusement park was powerfully lighted and fenced, and everyone present was a guest, we gave them permission. Two happier boys have never run into a wonderland. Before them lay every ride, all the food they could eat, games, sights, and splendor.

The party lasted from eight in the evening until midnight. We had arranged to meet the boys by the merry-go-round at a quarter to twelve. Of course, we saw them many times during the evening, always running to the next ride, their hands full of food, their eyes bright, eager, and a little greedy.

At the end of the evening, as we watched tired families stream toward the exit gates, our two exhausted little boys, their faces stained with chocolate and mustard, their feet dragging, and their heads almost lolling with weariness, walked up to us. My son looked into my eyes.

"I've learned something," he told me. "You know how I said I thought the best thing in the whole world would be when those gates opened? Nothing but party and fun!" He pointed toward the large gates at the entrance. I nodded. "Well, now," he said, "I think that the worst thing in this world would be if those gates closed and I couldn't leave."

It was absolutely one of the best evenings of his childhood, but he had also learned that pleasure has a timer, and when the timer rings, it ceases to be fun. It is then time to return to those basic things that give fun its meaning. Work gives purpose and importance to life, and that sense of purpose in all that we do is what turns fun into something more meaningful—into celebration.

Especially for women, the feeling of joy is consistently muddied by the sense of work undone. We wear our housework on our backs like a heavy burden, and the constant pressure we feel concerning the state of our homes robs us of the joy and pleasure we should be feeling.

For many of us, just opening our eyes in the morning brings an instant and oppressive realization of all the jobs that are waiting to pounce on us. Before our feet even touch the floor we are feeling overwhelmed and under the gun.

The thought of making life a celebration, of feeling joy, delight, interest, or happiness, seems like just one more job we have to do. No, thank you! we think. We put our heads down and work away, trying to do three jobs at once, snapping at the children to do their part, and worrying about the things that are slipping between the cracks. Our lives feel like a too-full basket of laundry we are trying to carry down a steep stairway, and things are just slipping and sliding and leaving a trail behind us.

I have found I need to do two things to control those oppressive feelings. The first is to look more consistently at what I *have* done than at what I have *not* done. No one else has to recognize what I have accomplished—it is enough that I do. The second thing is to realize that I have power over my own work. It is my opportunity to decide what needs to be done, and when, and how. I am the planner and the doer—and if things need to be changed or done better or differently, I have the power to think it through, to use my own initiative and decision.

For me, it was a day of celebration when I realized that a good deal of my work (not all of it, of course, but much of it) was my own choice. That sense of ownership of my work made homemaking seem more of a privilege, something to celebrate, and less like a punishment or an endless mountain I had to climb.

Most of us need to get rid of that "house mother" we carry around in our heads. You know the one—she judges everything we do—or don't do—and finds it wanting. Hers is the voice that says: "You must vacuum every day," or, "No one can come in unless your house is spotless," or, "You can't go for a walk if the laundry isn't done," or, "Don't let anyone know that sometimes you serve cold cereal for supper."

I don't know where this omnipresent arbiter with all her "musts" and "must nots" comes from. I suspect she is the echo of our mothers' voices from Saturday chores, but I also imagine that most of our mothers would be much less demanding and harsh than the voices in our heads that seem to judge and drive us.

If we are to use our work as the basis of a happier life, we have to take responsibility for it ourselves. We should begin to free ourselves from that overharsh internal voice. We set our own standards, make judgments, set priorities, and decide what needs to be done, what can be done, and how it shall be done. Valuing what we do and evaluating it creatively can bring us greater satisfaction.

One of my favorite stories tells of a village in Vietnam where the women had for centuries swept the floors and the streets with short-handled brooms. An American doctor noted that the women of that village were bent almost double, shuffling in exhausted old age by their early forties. As a scientist he was curious. Was it some rare form of osteoporosis? Was it their diet? Was it genetic? What caused this premature deformity?

He spent several days observing the life of the

village, watching as the women spent hours sweeping the mud and dirt of the fields and jungles from their doorsteps. He noted the awkward, stooping position they had to assume as they swept with their short-handled brooms, doing their assigned task of keeping the streets and houses of the village clean.

Finally the doctor asked an old woman, "Why do you sweep that way?"

"We have always used these brooms," she replied. "My mother, and her mother, and her mother before that. For as long as we have been a people. It is our tradition." The doctor gathered up the village brooms and replaced them with long-handled brooms.

Some of the women resisted the change. For some the new method of sweeping was difficult because they felt it was not right for them to stand comfortably upright when they were sweeping. It was too easy. They were meant to suffer. The wiser women, however, immediately saw how much better they could do their job—faster, more simply, with less effort and more control.

What a simple thing! Long-handled brooms changed lives of drudgery and despair into lives of dignity and health.

But I ask myself, why on earth didn't those women stop and analyze their job generations ago? They had the intellect and the power to have changed that terribly debilitating task themselves, but not one of those women had paused in her "duties" to stand back and analyze how her work could be done better, more joyfully, or with more sense of purpose.

All of us need to discover ways to put long-handled brooms into our own lives. In some ways we are all sweeping with short-handled brooms and feeling unnecessarily stressed and tired as a result. The secret to making our work a part of celebration is not to work harder but to find ways to add joy to the work we are doing, to claim our work with a greater sense of ownership and vigor.

A happily examined life can help us look at the things we do—regardless of our current life situation—and realize that we have power within us to do things better. We do not need to do more, just do what we are already doing in a more satisfying way. We need to create grace notes of celebration in the pattern of our work.

We need to feel in our minds that our work is ours to control. We are not controlled by it; we are not mindless. When my husband and I have bought new houses—which we have done more often than most because of the nature of my husband's career—I always say I need a home I can hold in my mind in one thought. I have to be able, in one image, to see the whole of the house in my mind and to know that I am capable of taking care of the entire home from edge to edge. I have to think my house through.

One excellent means of relieving ourselves of the guilt and stress of our labors is to develop habits of swift and consistent order. (Most of the illustrations I use involve housework, but the same principles apply to most work—career, community, volunteer, church, artistic.) When basic, habitual, daily order is established, then the rest of work can be balanced, performed, scheduled, prioritized, or dealt with expeditiously. A sense of basic order is fundamental. Here are a few tricks that have helped me establish that order.

• Make your bed the minute you rise—without thought, just as matter-of-factly as you brush your teeth.

• When you remove clothes, do not let them touch any surface but the place where they belong—hanger, drawer, laundry hamper, wherever. This same principle applies to mail and to laundry. Sort, stack, and discard on the spot. Try not to handle more than once anything that needs to be put away.

• Do dishes the same way. Clean up pots and implements as you prepare the meal. The minute the meal is finished, rinse and stack dishes in the machine, or wash them in hot, sudsy water, rinse in hotter water, wipe dry, and put away. Your kitchen is clean and ready for the next meal in just a few minutes.

If you stack the dishes in a drainer by the sink they may be clean, but they create clutter and represent an unfinished job. When you begin the next meal, the full dish drainer is usually still in the way. It takes only minutes to wipe the dishes and put them in the cupboard. Putting the dishes away immediately takes about half the time it takes to stack them, wait, and then finally put them away—that way you are handling them three times instead of once. Actually, I almost always do the dishes by hand for this reason, even though I have a dishwasher.

The Finnish people understand this principle. They have created cupboards with slotted racks and open slats on the bottom—over the sink—so that the washed dishes drain right in the cupboard. They have eliminated an entire step of the process.

• Work smarter, faster, more effectively. Analyze, set better priorities, and identify methods you use out of habit that are not truly productive.

Part of the joy of creating our home is that we have the right to choose how we want our home to be. If we are unhappy or uncomfortable about the way our home looks, or the way in which we are maintaining it, then *we must learn to believe that we are capable of making improvements.* In that belief, anticipation and effort can be real sources of happiness. The smallest improvement can create a sense of great celebration. An entire garden begins with one primrose.

If you would feel joy in your home, do not think of all the things you wish you could have—concentrate on what you can do to make things as they really are just a little better.

For example, a young student couple moved into their first home, a tiny, old pioneer house. The house seemed dark and old-fashioned to them, but they had no money to spend. With energy and a feeling of celebration, they pulled up the worn, ugly carpeting and discovered solid oak floors underneath. It took effort and time, but they sanded the floors, refinished them, and painted the walls of the house—and it became a splendid celebration of their dreams.

We should not let our failings, mistakes, or inadequacies discourage us. We are all in training—in fact, that is part of the fun. As long as I have lived I have felt the thrill of discovery as I have become aware of ways to improve how I do things. And I don't blame myself for things I don't know or have not done well. I figure I just have plenty of room left for learning.

For example, in the last two months I have learned how to make crustless quiche; I have found out how to roll out pie dough in plastic wrap, eliminating the mess; I have discovered that you should *never* carry a grocery bag with a bleach bottle in it across a carpet; I have just found out how to be a better mother to married children by thinking with praise; I have learned to write better by breaking old patterns—the list goes on and on. I rejoice in the lessons my work teaches me.

The following ideas are tools I have identified that help me keep my work and my life in basic order:

1. *Identify the real problem.* If something is troubling me about my home, it does not mean that I need to completely overhaul it. It does not mean that *everything* is wrong, that I am doing *nothing* right. It might simply mean that there is one thing out of control.

I think of one young mother who was always embarrassed when the visiting teachers came. "My house is such a mess!" she confided. I had been in her home. Of course there were toys on the floor from her toddlers, but the house was well-kept (and I personally think toys represent great homemaking).

As I talked with her she mentioned her frustration that there were always sticky handprints and dog-prints on the glass panes of her front door. It was the first thing people saw, and it made her ashamed.

The solution was easy. She decided to keep a small bottle of window cleaner by the front door, and first thing in the morning and last thing at night she whisked over the glass. Her front door sparkled. Nothing else was different, but in an instant her perception of herself as a homemaker was changed.

One good thing about celebratory change is that it can be done in small increments, in the midst of our daily life. Celebration is not the wardrobe of life, but it is the ribbon in the hair, the string of pearls, the flowers on the table, the grace notes that make the whole a delight.

2. *Deal with each task directly.* Sometimes we imagine we can put pending work out of our minds, but even when we think we have put off thinking about it, it

hovers in our mind like a dark cloud. A better way to handle work is to deal with it as quickly as possible.

There are three ways of dealing with a pending task: Do it. Plan it. Discard or delegate it.

I was a visitor in a ward for a few weeks recently, and I met a most remarkable woman who understood the principle of "do it." She introduced herself to us, invited us to dinner, planned an afternoon activity for another day, and organized a group of women to meet me.

Hers was a wonderful home, filled with all the evidence of a vibrant, active family, and yet filled also with a sense of order and accomplishment. When we went there for dinner I watched as she prepared the meal for us and her sizable family with swift, efficient hands. There was remarkable effortlessness in her manner as she simply did each task in an orderly fashion. The table was already set when we arrived, the vegetables were washed and ready, and the chicken was prepared for the grill.

For dessert we had fresh rhubarb preserves on ice cream. It struck me that this woman was the kind of person who, when the rhubarb was ripe, would not agonize, "Oh no, the rhubarb's ripe, and I'm so busy this week. How can I possibly find time to process it!" That would have been my complaint. But this remarkable woman would simply "do it." With matter-of-fact swiftness she would harvest, clean, and bottle the rhubarb, even if it meant a night or two of "working with a candle."

When something rises high enough in priority that it is in our minds and pressing on us constantly, the most joyful thing is simply to get it done and celebrate its completion.

The second alternative in dealing with a task is to *plan* when to do it. Many jobs hang over us like a nagging toothache: "I must get the windows washed." "I must get the ironing done." "My personal files are in complete disarray; I've got to get them organized." "I must go visit Aunt Lyla." Weeks go by, and the task looms over all our daily necessities. We may have absolutely no time to do that task, but it still nags away at us and spoils everything we are doing.

The way to remove such work from shadowing our happiness is to *plan* when we will do it. It is a remarkable phenomenon that specifically and definitely planning something gives us almost as much relief as getting it done.

Assign the day and the hours you will spend washing the windows two weeks from now. Write it down on your calendar as if it were any other appointment. Suddenly the grimy windows no longer nag or hang over you. You know that they are going to be cleaned.

Planning our work gives us power over our own agenda, and nothing gives more satisfaction in any kind of enterprise. When we plan the work, we are in charge of the job; the job is no longer in charge of us. That is empowerment, and it is essential to our feelings of celebration.

The third choice when we confront a task that is confronting us is to discard or delegate it.

Once I had a basket of ironing. My six little girls wore fluffy, full-skirted dresses and cotton blouses with puffed sleeves; this was in addition to the handkerchiefs, pillowcases, boys' shirts, tablecloths, and all the other sundry things we used to iron weekly in the years before permanent press.

At the end of one long afternoon of ironing, I had

finished most of the basket. The dresses, shirts, and linens were hung and stacked around the room, a great celebration of work accomplished. I was tired, but there were still several items at the bottom of the basket: dresses that were torn or had missing buttons, things the children seldom wore or had outgrown.

"Well," I thought (using my second method of handling a task), "I'll just plan to do the rest next week." Even though I had done a huge amount of ironing, I was not feeling much satisfaction. I continued to stare at the items I had not ironed.

I realized that those same clothes had been in the bottom of the basket for months—possibly for more than a year! It dawned on me that this pile of clothes had accumulated over many ironing days. The reason I had not ironed them was that they were basically unwearable—and ironing wasn't going to make them any more wearable. Some misguided inner voice had been telling me I "ought" to iron them.

With a moment's reflection I realized that if we had gone without those clothes for more than a year, we could obviously do without them for good.

I tore up the bottom-of-the-basket clothes for cleaning rags and put them in my broom cupboard. For the first time in months my ironing basket was completely empty, and I felt great!

When discarding or delegating—jettisoning—a job is appropriate, do not hesitate to do so.

When we are homemakers, we also must consider the attitudes and needs of our husbands and children. Husbands come in all varieties, as do children, and our work is influenced by their expectations and demands. The arts of negotiation and consideration are important aspects of our job.

As we perform, plan, and discard or delegate our tasks, we should be certain that we have considered our relationships with others. We will probably encounter differences of opinion or feelings that labor is not fairly shared. We need to learn to organize, to negotiate, and to express our feelings and approaches to the tasks that must be performed.

Relationships can definitely affect the way in which we work and how we feel about it—and some of those issues might take time to resolve. Still, the principles of work should improve our ability to perform our labors and to create an atmosphere of order, no matter what pressures and challenges we face in our individual circumstances. Try making small improvements in your approach and methods, and you will be surprised what a building thing even small increments of change can be.

3. *Use better tools.* Hunt for the best bathroom cleaner you can find—one that does the scrubbing for you and removes the mildew and soap scum through cleanser reaction. Keep looking until you find it.

Let hot water and time work on your side. Soak food-encrusted pans and stained objects. Use rubber gloves so that you can use stronger cleansers and hotter water.

Use sharper knives, a good vacuum (a really good vacuum can do bare floors as well as carpet, and cleans better than a broom), good laundry detergents, and heavy-duty, quality pots and pans. Purchase them one at a time if necessary. A good pan will save its cost in food that is not burned or ruined.

4. *Listen and learn from others in your profession.* Don't be reluctant to talk about your work. When you see a job that is wonderfully well done, ask questions about

the methods, tools, and approaches used to accomplish it.

I have learned a few things from asking or observing other women: how to remove spots on the carpet with club soda; how to plant bare-root roses (what a great experience that was. I thought, as I did it, "Plant a stick—get a stick," but just as I was promised by my friend, the bushes grew and bloomed gloriously); how to use pattern and color in my house; how to hang pictures; how to arrange flowers; how to organize my linen closet; how to use a computer more effectively; and dozens of other ways to accomplish work more joyfully.

5. *Turn work itself into celebration.* Learn ways to make work more fun, both mentally and actually. I do absolutely love to work. I love the touch, the feel, the effort, and the completion of my labors. Some jobs I like better than others, but there are elements of celebration in everything I do.

In contemplating the symbiotic relationship of joy and work, I wrote the following poem.

AN UNFINISHED WOMAN

Here am I, Lord,
The dishes barely done and night long since fallen,
The children would not go to bed
And would not go and
Would not go—
And now they are gone.
Gone to places of their own with children of their own
Who will not go to bed and will not go . . .
And I have taught them what I could and
They have learned the things they would
And now they've gone their way alone to learn the rest
Most on their own.

And I remain, not half spent.
And I remain, not yet content,
So much to do, so much to learn,
So much to feel, so much to yearn.
My past mistakes make stepping-stones,
Not millstones great around my neck but
Stones to guide my searching feet—
And I must search; I'm incomplete.

I watch my years go tumbling by
And I must use them better, I
Have yet so much to learn and do
Before I can return to You.

The hour is late. The night comes on,
My celestial self I would become.
Ah! What wisdom thou gavest to mortal life—

I,
As sister, mother, daughter, wife—
In earthly roles have seen Thy face.
In my womanly life Thy heavenly place
Is taught through humble tasks and pain.
So, if royal robes I would obtain,
To wear as all Thy glories burst—
I'll need to do the laundry first.

One of the sweetest things about work is that when we live with the habits of basic order, we can occasionally give ourselves permission to play truant from daily chores. Once in a while it is a source of sheer celebratory joy to run out of the house with our children to catch the morning breeze at the beach, or kick the soccer ball at the park, or go to see the new puppies at the neighbors', leaving the dishes in the sink, the laundry in the hamper, and the cobwebs in the corners. Work will hold, but certain opportunities for joy are as brief as the wink of a firefly and must be grasped on the instant.

A life of basic order gives us the courage to make the choice to fly free because we know our string is tethered.

I wandered lonely as a cloud
That floats on high o'er vales and hills,
When all at once I saw a crowd,
A host, of golden daffodils.

William Wordsworth, 1770–1850

2

The Daffodil Principle

Several times my daughter had telephoned to say, "Mother, you must come see the daffodils before they are over." I wanted to go, but it was a two-hour drive from Laguna to Lake Arrowhead. Going and coming took most of a day—and I honestly did not have a free day until the following week.

"I will come next Tuesday," I promised, a little reluctantly, on her third call.

Next Tuesday dawned cold and rainy. Still, I had promised, and so I drove the length of Route 91, continued on I-215, and finally turned onto Route 18 and began to drive up the mountain highway.

The tops of the mountains were sheathed in clouds, and I had gone only a few miles when the road was completely covered with a wet, gray blanket of fog. I slowed to a crawl, my heart pounding.

The road becomes narrow and winding toward the top of the mountain. As I executed the hazardous turns at a snail's pace, I was praying to reach the turnoff at Blue Jay that would signify I had arrived.

When I finally walked into Carolyn's house and

hugged and greeted my grandchildren, I said, "Forget the daffodils, Carolyn! The road is invisible in the clouds and fog, and there is nothing in the world except you and these darling children that I want to see bad enough to drive another inch!"

My daughter smiled calmly. "We drive in this all the time, Mother."

"Well, you won't get *me* back on the road until it clears—and then I'm heading for home!" I assured her.

"I was hoping you'd take me over to the garage to pick up my car. The mechanic just called, and they've finished repairing the engine," she answered.

"How far will we have to drive?" I asked cautiously.

"Just a few blocks," Carolyn said cheerfully. So we bundled up the children and went out to my car. "I'll drive," Carolyn offered. "I'm used to this."

We got into the car, and she began driving. In a few minutes I was aware that we were back on the Rim-of-the-World road heading over the top of the mountain.

"Where are we going?" I exclaimed, distressed to be back on the mountain road in the fog. "This isn't the way to the garage!"

"We're going to my garage the long way," Carolyn smiled, "by way of the daffodils."

"Carolyn," I said sternly, trying to sound as if I were still the mother and in charge of the situation, "please turn around. There is nothing in the world that I want to see enough to drive on this road in this weather."

"It's all right, Mother," she replied with a knowing grin. "I know what I'm doing. I promise, you will never forgive yourself if you miss this experience."

And so my sweet, darling daughter who had never given me a minute of difficulty in her whole life was suddenly in charge—and she was kidnapping me! I couldn't believe it. Like it or not, I was on the way to see some ridiculous daffodils—driving through the thick, gray silence of the mist-wrapped mountaintop at what I thought was risk to life and limb. I muttered all the way.

After about twenty minutes we turned onto a small gravel road that branched down into an oak-filled hollow on the side of the mountain. The fog had lifted a little, but the sky was lowering, gray and heavy with clouds. We parked in a small parking lot adjoining a little stone church. From our vantage point at the top of the mountain we could see beyond us, in the mist, the crests of the San Bernardino range like the dark, humped backs of a herd of elephants. Far below us the fog-shrouded valleys, hills, and flatlands stretched away to the desert.

On the far side of the church I saw a pine-needle–covered path, with towering evergreens and manzanita bushes and an inconspicuous, hand-lettered sign, "Daffodil Garden."

We each took a child's hand, and I followed Carolyn down the path as it wound through the trees. The mountain sloped away from the side of the path in irregular dips, folds, and valleys, like a deeply creased skirt. Live oaks, mountain laurel, shrubs, and bushes clustered in the folds, and in the gray, drizzling air, the green foliage looked dark and monochromatic. I shivered. Then we turned a corner of the path, and I looked up and gasped.

Before me lay the most glorious sight, unexpectedly and completely splendid. It looked as though someone had taken a great vat of gold and poured it down over the mountain peak and slopes, where it had run into every crevice and over every rise. Even in the mist-filled air, the mountainside was radiant, clothed in massive drifts and waterfalls of daffodils. The flowers were planted in majestic, swirling patterns, great ribbons and swaths of deep orange, white, lemon yellow, salmon pink, saffron, and butter yellow. Each different-colored variety (I learned later that there were more than thirty-five varieties of daffodils in the vast display) was planted as a group so that it swirled and flowed like its own river with its own unique hue.

In the center of this incredible and dazzling display of gold, a great cascade of purple grape hyacinth flowed down like a waterfall of blossoms framed in its own rock-lined basin, weaving through the brilliant daffodils. A charming path wound throughout the garden. There were several resting stations, paved with stone and furnished with Victorian wooden benches and great tubs of coral and carmine tulips.

As though this were not magnificence enough, Mother Nature had to add her own grace note—above the daffodils, a bevy of western bluebirds flitted and darted, flashing their brilliance. These charming little birds are the color of sapphires with breasts of magenta red. As they dance in the air, their colors are truly like jewels. Above the blowing, glowing daffodils, the effect was spectacular.

It did not matter that the sun was not shining. The brilliance of the daffodils was like the glow of the brightest sunlit day. Words, wonderful as they are, simply cannot describe the incredible beauty of that flower-bedecked mountaintop.

Five acres of flowers! (This too I discovered later when some of my questions were answered.) "But who has done this?" I asked Carolyn. I was overflowing with gratitude that she had brought me—even against my will. This was a once-in-a-lifetime experience. "Who?" I asked again, almost speechless with wonder, "and how, and why, and when?"

"It's just one woman," Carolyn answered. "She lives on the property. That's her home." Carolyn pointed to a well-kept A-frame house that looked small and modest in the midst of all that glory.

We walked up to the house, my mind buzzing with questions. On the patio we saw a poster. "Answers to the Questions I Know You Are Asking" was the headline. The first answer was a simple one. "50,000 bulbs," it read. The second answer was, "One at a time, by one woman. Two hands, two feet, and very little brain." The third answer was, "Began in 1958."

There it was. The Daffodil Principle. For me that moment was a life-changing experience. I thought of this woman whom I had never met, who, more than thirty-five years before, had begun—one bulb at a time—to bring her vision of beauty and joy to an obscure mountaintop.

One bulb at a time. There was no other way to do it. One bulb at a time. No shortcuts—simply loving the slow process of planting. Loving the work as it unfolded. Loving an achievement that grew so slowly and that bloomed for only three weeks of each year.

Still, just planting one bulb at a time, year after year, had changed the world. This unknown woman had forever changed the world in which she lived. She had created something of ineffable magnificence, beauty, and inspiration.

The principle her daffodil garden taught me is one

of the greatest principles of celebration: learning to move toward our goals and desires one step at a time—often just one baby-step at a time—learning to love the doing, learning to use the accumulation of time. When we multiply tiny pieces of time with small increments of daily effort, we too will find we can accomplish magnificent things. We can change the world.

A friend of mine began years ago to save one dollar a week in a special account. Whenever she bought groceries, she put an extra dollar in her account. She started this practice from the first week she was married. She put away just that little bit of money at a time, but she did it regularly and through many years.

As the family became more affluent, she increased the amount to five dollars, to ten, and finally to twenty-five a week. Each time she wrote a check for groceries, she wrote the small check for her savings account. Through the years the consistent week-by-week saving added up and earned its own interest. Time plus consistent small effort multiplied into a valuable gift of security for herself and her family.

Another friend has just completed her studies for a doctorate in music pedagogy. She has four children, has been Relief Society president, and maintains a full and active life. "How did you do it?" I asked her.

"I will tell you the truth," she replied. "About eight years ago I had to teach a lesson in Relief Society on time management, and I read and taught the concept of 'five minutes a day' to the women. I taught the concept so well that I believed it myself.

"I had lots of really little children at that time, but I enrolled in graduate school and began my classes—

and I maintained my school work with a consistent 'five minutes a day.' I could not believe how much that little amount of time, used consistently toward a single goal, could accomplish!" All those five minutes a day over the years have added up to a doctorate.

The trick to living with celebration is to enjoy the one-at-a-time part of it as well as the final goal. I remember watching a friend tile a bathroom. I looked at the whole room and wondered how he would ever finish it.

He knew exactly what he was going to do. He had already made the decisions about patterns and colors. Now, as he worked, never looked around to see how much there was left to do or how much he had accomplished.

There was no impatience in him or frustration. He simply picked up each individual tile, and, working at a careful, precise pace, he made certain that each single tile—the tile he was working on at each moment—was put in place perfectly.

The bathroom slowly began to be transformed. He was enjoying the work, the pace, and the moment. In two days, he stepped back to admire the completed room. He had done only one tile at a time, but he had done it flawlessly and continuously. One unhurried tile at a time had created a beautiful room.

The important thing to remember is that in the celebration of life, magnificent things are accomplished with small, consistent, daily acts that build through time into all the great achievements that change our lives—and change the world.

We can set great goals, and then, with a pattern of patient, consistent, careful effort—if only for minutes a day—we can eventually achieve our goals.

Pablo Casals, arguably the greatest cellist of this century, died in his ninth decade. On the day of his death, he spent the early hours of the morning practicing his scales. He had become a great cellist one day at a time—a lifetime of one day at a time.

Choose great enterprises and work toward them in the midst of the fray—just one bulb at a time. Those few minutes each day spent working toward a larger goal give the repetitive actions of our lives a fresh aspect.

I wrote my first novel when the youngest of my twelve children started kindergarten. I simply kept my typewriter in the kitchen and wrote for a few minutes a day every time I could find the time.

That year my husband was traveling 80 percent of the time, I had nine children at home—and no household help—my first two grandchildren were born, I was teaching seminary and doing the ward roadshow and being active on several PTA and community boards. When I read my journal of that period, I find it hard to know how I possibly found the time to place all those words, one letter at a time, onto paper.

At the end of an entry in March, in which I speak of a sick child, household guests, a church assignment, and my husband's trip—is this observation: "Today, I wrote the last sentence of my book."

It isn't enough just to turn our one-at-a-time efforts into a future event of celebration. We must learn to rejoice in the daily steps as well as in the anticipation of the far-off goal. How many vacation trips are spoiled for our children because they spend their time asking, "When will we get there?" All that seems important to them about the trip is the arriving. The glories of the world are passing by their eyes in the windows of the car, but all they can ask is when will they arrive!

We sometimes live our lives in just the same way. We are so eager to get to the final accomplishments that we forget to enjoy the process of achieving them. If our trip is well begun, well planned, and in the direction we desire, then each turn of the wheels, each step of the hike, each push of the bicycle wheel should be a joy along the way and will add up to arrival at our destination. Impatience for the goal will not speed the steps. The very best, most celebratory way to live is to enjoy each day's journey as well as its arrivals. Choose great goals and work toward them patiently, consistently. Let time and increments of progress work together to accomplish mighty things.

When I was a little girl in Canada, I remember visiting a friend at her home. It was early twilight, and my mother phoned to tell me it was time to come home for supper. Because it was dusk, I did not want to walk alone, and I asked my friend's mother if she could walk with me.

"It is such a long way to my house!" I complained to her. (I think, actually, it was about two blocks, but it seemed a long way.)

"I'm sorry, dear," the mother told me, "you must go alone. We are going to eat our supper. It is not far, Jaroldeen, and you have done it many times."

She could see I was still reluctant, unhappy, and a little fearful.

"Don't be worried," she reassurred me. "You don't have to think how far it is. All you need to do is take the next step. Just know where you are going, and then concentrate on picking up your back foot and putting it in front of your other foot. Do that. Just think about the next step, and the next. You will be at your home before you know it."

It was years before I got over my amazement at how well her advice worked! I concentrated on lifting up my foot and putting it in front of the other, and suddenly, I looked up and I was home!

"Carolyn," I said that morning on the top of the mountain as we left the haven of daffodils, our minds and hearts still bathed and bemused by the splendors we had seen, "it's as though that remarkable woman has needle-pointed the earth! Decorated it. Just think of it, she planted every single bulb. For more than thirty years. One bulb at a time! And that's the only way this garden could be created. Every individual bulb had to be planted. There was no way of short-circuiting that process. Five acres of blooms. That magnificent cascade of hyacinth! All, all, just one bulb at a time." The thought of it filled my mind. I was suddenly overwhelmed with the implications of what I had seen.

"It makes me sad in a way," I admitted to Carolyn. "What might I have accomplished if I had thought of a wonderful goal thirty-five years ago and had worked away at it 'one bulb at a time' through all those years. Just think what I might have been able to achieve!"

My wise daughter put the car into gear and summed up the message of the day in her direct way. "Start tomorrow," she said with the same knowing smile she had worn for most of the morning. Oh, profound wisdom! It is pointless to think of the lost hours of yesterdays. The way to make learning a lesson a celebration instead of a cause for regret is to only ask, "How can I put this to use tomorrow?"

I also learned on that gray and golden morning what a blessing it is to have a child who is not a child anymore but a woman—perceptive and loving beyond her years—and to be humble in that awareness.

Thank you, Carolyn. Thank you for the lessons of that unforgettable morning. Thank you for the gift of the daffodils.

I cleaned the windows and I swept the floor
And I polished up the handle of the big front door.
I polished up the handle so carefullee
That now I am the Ruler of the Queen's Navee!

Sir William S. Gilbert, 1836–1911

3

···

The Last 3 Percent

I remember hearing as a child the nursery rhyme that began, "For want of a nail the shoe was lost; for want of the shoe, the horse was lost; for want of the horse the battle was lost." I recall feeling sad, because it seemed to me such an unfair thing to lose the whole battle just because someone forgot to put in a nail.

In the years since childhood, I have come to know that much of our joy and satisfaction depends on the way in which we complete the last 3 percent of our responsibilities. That vital last 3 percent consists of three things: 1 percent is the final detail of work; 1 percent is the way we feel and think about what we have done—our reasons, motivations and satisfactions; and the last 1 percent consists of original and creative thinking with which we crown the finished product.

It has been said that genius is an infinite capacity for taking pains. Much of the work and many of the activities in which we take part we do out of duty in habitual ways—but if we are to intensify our awareness and delight in our life, then we should assess how we can multiply the effect of ordinary and repetitive events.

How often when our children set the table do they consider the job finished when the plates, glasses, and cutlery are set out? True, at that point they have done most of the work—but the job is not finished. That last percent of effort—the napkins, the water, the salt, pepper, and butter—must be in place before the job is really and truly and happily finished. That last 1 percent of effort added to the bulk of the work makes the table complete and comfortable.

That last small quantum of work primarily holds the gift of satisfaction in it. The finishing details give us the confidence that we have done well—that we have carried our work to the level of loving service.

In the satisfaction that comes from work well completed, the most common tasks are enhanced. In that last small fraction of extra effort, we also think of ways to make the moment memorable (for example, adding to the table candles, or napkins folded a new way, or funny place cards, or a newspaper tablecloth, or fresh flowers, etc.). Then the last 3 percent of effort has made an ordinary, everyday chore into a moment of genuine celebration.

Training ourselves to do the last essential fraction of work is an extremely important skill. In professional settings it is called task completion and is one of the most important measures of an effective employee. The concept of task completion is essential to success in any field.

Many people work extremely hard and for long hours. They work hours and hours and feel that as long as they are working, work is being accomplished. Of course it is, but that does not mean that essential tasks are being completed. Work alone does not mean that the job is getting done.

Working without the skills of finishing the last essential part is like a carpenter hammering nails into a board but with no concept of what he is building—and no way of knowing how to finish. He is working, but the work is not leading to accomplishment or celebration. It becomes drudgery.

Think of all the college students who write letter after letter home but do not get the letter into a stamped envelope and into the mail. The truth is, an unsent letter is not a letter, because, although writing the letter is most of the work, the small but essential finishing effort has not been done. And so the work is barren.

When we understand the last-3-percent principle, we see to it that we have stamps and envelopes on hand, and we are sure to finish the essential act of letter-writing, which is *to mail the letter.*

Identifying the essential final fraction of effort that is required for task completion is an important skill. It is the putting away of the vacuum; it is the putting away of the folded laundry; it is the attractive cover on a school report; it is the books thoughtfully placed on the night table in the guest room; it is the clean towels in the clean bathroom; it is the thank-you note written and sent. It is fresh fragrances in a tidy house; it is candy in the pockets; it is the wreath on the door; it is the timely visit to the sick; it is writing with a pen you love to hold; it is remembered birthdays; it is cleaning up after the cookies are made.

Frequently our ability to rejoice, to use our creativity, to feel our own abilities, uniqueness, and effectiveness—our opportunity to celebrate—is contained in those last precious moments of effort and thought. When everyone else would have quit, walked away from the job, left it till another day, or said, "Good enough is good enough," the celebratory worker keeps on going for the few extra moments which make all the difference.

I have watched young women work tremendously hard to clean and organize their house. They work from dawn until dusk without pause—and when the day is finished, nothing looks different because they leave a path of clutter in their wake. The end result is frustration and despair.

It would be better for them to work less hard physically, to pause in their work and ask, "What must I do to give my home the appearance of orderliness? What is keeping it from feeling and looking organized?" In other words, "What do I need to do to make my work achieve its objectives?" Almost always, the answer will be something that is only a small part of the huge job of cleaning the home. It may be a large basket into which all the toys can be thrown, so that the room is uncluttered. It may be that the dishes need to be put into the cupboards. It may be that a clutter of magazines and papers needs to be organized, put away in drawers or baskets, or discarded. It may be that rooms need to be rearranged.

So often, when we have worked hard, we are tired and bored as a chore reaches its end, and we are tempted to shrug our shoulders at the last ounce of effort. "The clothes are washed, and I'm too tired to fold them and put them away. I'll leave them in the basket and do them first thing in the morning." A day ends with a basket of laundry in the family room or laundry room, and often the children get at it and scatter the clean clothes—more mess—or it gets mixed up with the unwashed laundry, and the sense of being overwhelmed is added upon. The sad part is, the last part is only a fraction of the long job of washing, drying, and folding the clothes. But that last ounce of effort makes all the work that has gone before satisfying and complete.

Closing the cupboard doors, taking out the garbage, picking up the dirty dishtowels, adding bleach to the load of whites—these are the final details that give us a sense of joy, empowerment, and celebration in our work.

It is in the details that we know we are doing it well. Those details create much of the celebration of our daily life.

Identifying the essential part of each task is an important part of working with joy. Sometimes we can learn to short-circuit the bulky part of the work and finish the job more quickly by judiciously attending to the most significant features. For example, I know that the cleanest house will not look clean with clutter in it, and so I have established a simple motto: "Leave every room looking better than when you entered it." Pick up as you go. That is true not just of housework—it is true of any pursuit.

"Picking up" is usually part of the "last 3 percent," but if it is done consistently and regularly, we have shortened all phases of every project.

The difference between excellent and good, between job satisfaction and feeling overwhelmed, between success and failure is often the result of a very small proportion of effort and creative thought. Benjamin Franklin spoke of the misery of the person who has one dollar and spends one dollar and a penny. He contrasted that with the plenty, happiness, and joy of the person who has one dollar and spends ninety-nine cents. The difference between sorrow and happiness—just two cents.

Our happiness is bound up in the final fraction of effort, in the determination not just to endure to the end but to add one last touch of glory. When we fail to continue through that last bit of commitment, we often miss the mark—and all our effort toward happy enterprises can be lost by our having neglected the final small things. Life then becomes a series of disappointments rather than celebrations.

The "last 3 percent" is a principle of hope because it helps us understand that joy and success are often within our ready reach. With more wisdom, effort, creativity, and hope, we can discover those fine differences that will help us make the substance of our lives a little more divine. Things that we are currently doing with little satisfaction may, with an extra fraction of effort, become sources of real delight in our ordinary, daily lives.

One of my children had a report on Brazil that was due in her fourth-grade social studies class. She had done excellent work in compiling the information and writing the report. Each section of the report had a heading—geography, agriculture, wildlife, arts, and so on. "We're supposed to have some pictures or visual aids with the report, Mother," she told me.

"Shall I help you find some magazines or maps that we could use to cut out pictures?" I asked.

"No," she said. "I want to draw my own, but I want to do them with my colored chalks."

She loved to draw, and I had recently purchased a box of pastels. My first impulse was to suggest that the chalks wouldn't work because the colors would rub off. Then I remembered that in portfolios of pastels, a tissue is placed in front of the chalk-drawings to protect the colors from imprinting the other pages. I suggested that she do the drawings and then place a sheet of tissue paper between the drawing and the page of text. Then we could staple it all together like a book.

She drew maps, toucans, rubber trees, boats, and Brazilian designs. Each illustration was a full page and faced the page on which the report of that subject was written. Between the two pages we put a delicate page of tissue paper. Suddenly, an ordinary child's report took on the aspect of something precious and wonderful. The tissue, just like the tissue that wraps a fine piece of china, or a beautiful dress in its box, elevated the whole project to a different level of creative delight.

Such a little thing—just hanging in with the last 3 percent, and yet this child, now grown to a splendid young woman, still remembers that report. That one small experience taught her delight in the experience of learning—and from it sprang years of wonderful to-the-last-drop schooling. She is a terrific and remarkable student.

From my youngest son I learned the principle in serving others. For his Eagle project he decided to create a library in the Church camp on a lake in upstate New York. It was a two-hour drive from our home to the camp.

William's goal was to take a small, abandoned cabin, clean it, paint it, carpet it, build shelves, and conduct a book drive to fill them. We made several trips to the camp with as many members of the troop as possible and worked on the small building until it was painted inside and out and the new carpeting and shelves were installed.

By now, we were all—except William—beginning to lose enthusiasm for the project. The round-trip drive was getting longer and longer. Nonetheless, for what I hoped was the last time, I drove him and one stalwart friend with the boxes of collected books up to the camp. The trim on the windows and the front porch of the cabin still needed to be painted green, and the books needed to be placed on the shelves. While the boys painted outside, I emptied the boxes of books. The library looked wonderful—clean, inviting, and everything William could have wished. I was sure that many a child would spend happy hours and rain-washed days sitting in its pleasant comfort, lost in the pages of some wonderful books.

It was late in the day, and I was anxious to return home. As I walked outside the cabin I saw William's friend heading down to the lake. Even he had had enough and was calling it good.

William was climbing down from a ladder. He had just finished painting the last window trim.

"Are we ready to go?" I asked.

"Not quite," William replied. "I have to sand down the steps and paint them. It's the last thing that must be done."

I, like William's friend, felt my patience run out. "Honey," I said, "Everything is wonderful—it's just great. You've done more than anyone could have expected. It's so late, and we are all so tired. The steps just aren't important."

William paused for a moment. "They are to me, Mother. You see, this is my Eagle project—it's a gift I'm giving, and I don't want to remember every time I think of it through the years that I didn't finish the steps."

We painted the steps and drove home through the dark.

It is important to understand, as William did, that if a certain detail will improve the completion of the task or the event and we do not do it, the memory of the unfinished detail will always take some of the celebration out of the achievement.

Another example of the joys of the last 3 percent was demonstrated to me by another daughter. I was busy canning peaches when a neighbor called to ask if my five-year-old daughter could go over to play. I asked my twelve-year-old to escort her little sister to the neighbor's house. Robin said she'd be happy to, and the two little girls walked out of the kitchen. A few minutes later they were back, and my five-year-old came up to kiss me good-bye. I looked at her. Her older sister had washed her face and hands, had brushed and braided her hair, and put a bright red bow in it. Patricia looked as fresh, loved, and pretty as a child could look. Just a few minutes of effort, but what a difference. Not only had Robin agreed to take her sister to the neighbor's house but she had envisioned the last 3 percent of the job and taken the time to make her sister look like the wonderful guest she was! In doing the last fraction she had given all three of us a moment of genuine celebration.

Life itself is a whole piece of work—and therefore we should contemplate what the last 3 percent of completing it well must be. There should be wonderful goals we have saved for our later years. And if we are privileged to have children under our care, each day, each moment we should be looking for the essential

part of our efforts, the part that will give them meaning and crown those child-rearing years with celebration. Often at the end of a long, hard day of caring for
our families, it is easy to think we are too tired for family prayer, too tired to read a story, too tired to sit by a
bedside and whisper words of love and sharing. These
things take such a little extra effort, and yet they are
the part that makes all the rest meaningful.

When we recognize the minute gap that separates
ordinary accomplishment from accomplishment that
gives satisfaction and joy, we can feel a tremendous
surge of hope, because we understand that by seeing
our lives with new eyes, we can identify little things
that can lift our spirits, our memories, and our ability
to rejoice in work nobly completed. Everyday occa-
sions can be transformed into experiences of joy. The
power of improving the delight of our lives is not an
enormous thing—it is a small proportion of all the
hundreds of things we are already doing right.

To make room for the satisfying 3 percent, we can
find ways to throw out or cut through, some of the
mass of stuff that comes in the regular work. For example, after hours spent on preparing a lesson or a
speech, as I begin work on the visual aids, I could
spend more hours trying to impress my listeners with
the professional quality of the lettering on my posters
or word strips. I ask myself, "What is the essential
3 percent of visual aids?" My answer is that they are to
enhance the quality of learning, nothing more.
Therefore, I spend time thinking of ideas for visual
aids that will truly illustrate the points of my lesson.
That is the essential part. I spend no time at all on
worrying about the posters looking impressive. It is
the ideas that must be impressive—and the visual

aids must have originality and flair that seize the imagination.

I use original and unexpected things, such as long rolls of brown paper stretched across the room with time lines or sequences of events or biography tacked clear across the front of the classroom with my ever-present reusable adhesive, one of my essential 3 percents. How many teachers have you seen with wonderful visual aids who spend half their lesson time trying to get the visual aids to stay up on the wall or board—and they fall down inopportunely, interrupting the spirit of the lesson? The frustrated teacher has put much work into the visual aids but has forgotten the last, important little detail: an easy and effective way to secure them. This is a very good example of how the final, small details hold the key to success and celebration.

The last 3 percent is like a kiss at the end of the day. All the long labors of our day are the affirmation and evidence of our dedication and affection for others, but the kiss makes it all glow.

The ability to simplify means to eliminate the unnecessary
so that the necessary may speak.

Hans Hoffmann, 1880–1966

4

The Poached-Pears
Principle

$\mathcal{R}$eading cookbooks is something I enjoy very much. I also like cooking demonstrations, and so I invited the women whom I visit teach to come with me to a small cooking school to have lunch and learn how to make the foods we were served.

The dessert turned out to be poached pears—each pear like a jeweled, perfect gift, sitting in crème fraîche and topped with a mint leaf, as though the deep purple pear (steeped in blueberry nectar so the white flesh of the peeled pear had turned a rich amethyst color) still sported its own, fresh-picked leaf.

Pears are a very simple item, but poaching turns them into something magical.

That evening I talked about poached pears and built anticipation, and, at the end of the meal, I served poached pears for dessert.

My family and I felt we had eaten at a king's table. I did not have to cook a banquet to make them feel I had given them a banquet.

The principle of simplifying our life helps us to jettison outworn habits, unimportant klederments (a Southern word for stuff that accumulates and hangs on to us), and old, wasteful ways of doing things.

Simplification also teaches us to evaluate that which is important and essential against that which is busy-work or things done only to impress others.

As we try to simplify our lives, we need to look for worthwhile, exciting, and wonderful ways to fill the spaces that we open up. Lillian Gilbreth, the mother in *Cheaper by the Dozen*, was an efficiency engineer. She said that when a new child was born, she made it a policy to throw one outgrown thing out of her life and to let in more sunshine.

The real purpose of simplification is to fill our lives with activities that build joy—pondering, savoring, concentrating on others, conversing, studying, and appreciating the gifts and blessings that surround us.

When our lives are too complex, we have no time to refine them.

So often we think that changes in our lives must be elaborate or that celebratory events cannot occur without having sweep and scope, without time and money, without complicated step-by-step patterns. As we learn the uses of simplification we find that focused simplicity can give even more happiness than elaborate and tradition-encrusted events.

I use simplicity to add joy and celebration to our daily experience of eating. Mealtimes should be one of the great centers of celebration in family life—convivial, lovely, nourishing to both body and heart—a time of savoring.

Now I know that some meals are rushed and full of stress and just a lot of work. But I also know that with wise and creative care and simplification, most meals can be more filled with celebration and wonder.

For their afternoon meal, farm workers in France will pick a head of cauliflower, steam it whole, marinate the tender florets in oil and vinegar with herbs and Parmesan cheese, and, with a loaf of fresh, crusty bread, make that their entire meal.

My family has tried it—and it is not only delicious but such a delightful break from traditional meals. That simple meal is an experience that helps us savor one flavor to the fullest, to think of the bounties and variety of the harvest of this earth, and to feel a shared delight with unknown workers in a distant land.

At the height of strawberry season, or asparagus season, or corn season, or artichoke season, we have often made our entire meal of the single delicious variety of fruit or vegetable. I remember my father saying once, as my mother rationed out the strawberry short-cake, "Strawberry season is so short—don't you think that just once during the season everyone should have absolutely as many strawberries as he could possibly want?"

A few weeks later we drove across the border from Canada to Kalispell, Montana, and on the way home we bought a flat of strawberries at a roadside stand. We had only a couple of hours' drive back to the border, and we could not take any produce back into Canada, so we ate strawberries until we could scarcely swallow.

Most of the family fell asleep, but I was sitting in the front seat talking to my father. He was still eating strawberries, and the border was getting closer and closer. Any berries that were left would be confiscated. I watched his hand as it reached up to the dashboard to choose a berry from the box that was balanced there. He would eat the strawberry, savor it, and then in a minute, his hand would reach out again.

Finally his hand hovered for a good thirty seconds and then returned to the steering wheel—empty.

"Well," my father muttered to himself, "I have finally, for once in my life, had all the strawberries I can eat."

If we are to simplify our homes, our lives, and the work we do, it is very important to know ourselves. No two people will ever simplify in the same way because things that are unnecessary complications to one person may be a joy to another.

I have two friends to whom laundry is the most delightful chore of homemaking. Their laundry rooms are marvels, and they delight in the entire process.

I, on the other hand, have spent decades quite successfully figuring out methods of simplifying, short-cutting, and minimizing the job of laundry in my household because it is such a huge and, for me, an unbeloved task. I do delight in sparkling white linens, fresh towels, and clean, clean dishcloths, however, so I have learned to accomplish the work but in its most efficient and simplified form.

I do laundry early and late in the day. I use soft water, bleach, and excellent detergents. I have large, industrial-size machines.

I have laundry baskets everywhere, and because my home does not have a laundry chute, I throw the clothes over the banister from the second floor so I do not have to carry the loads downstairs.

Then I gather up the clothes immediately, sort them in the laundry room, and run a load morning and night.

Clothes are folded on the couch in my upstairs bedroom because most of them are put away on the second floor. I fold rapidly and always have a second activity going while I am folding—someone to talk to me, homework to discuss, a tape or a program playing.

Tricky items I take to the cleaners. Before I buy anything I ask myself, "How hard will this be to keep clean?" and, if the answer is "very hard" or "very expensive," I don't buy it.

The best clue to knowing when we should do a simplification assessment of our life is when we begin to feel that something is too much for us.

When we find ourselves worrying almost daily about a certain obligation—a church calling, or a household chore, or a commitment we have made— then that is a clue that we need to look for areas in our life in which we are using our time and energy ineffectively. We have let our lives become encrusted with clutter.

It happens to everyone, and we just need to look for the clues to tell us to stop and evaluate what changes would help.

I had fallen into the habit, without realizing it, of going to the store every day for a few items. We lived close to the store, and it had become easy to run over in the late afternoon to pick up a few little extras for dinner.

When the bishop called me to be Young Women president, I was suddenly faced with staggering new demands on my time. Quickly it became apparent that those minutes I spent each day at the grocery store were adding up to a considerable amount of time in the week.

That habit was the first to go. Now I manage with

what I buy in one hour on Saturday morning. Shopping has been simplified and condensed, and the gift of time is amazing.

In simplifying our lives and those of our children it is extremely important to savor and love the simple delights. Simple things are sweet, but savoring simple things takes a great spirit that understands the concept of life as a celebration.

To fully appreciate simplicity we need clear, trained eyes that see magnificence in simple things, and a pure heart that recognizes the hand of the Lord in a blade of grass.

One of my daughters married a young man who is attending Columbia Law School in New York City. They are living on a student's budget. As we visited on the telephone not long ago I asked what they had done for the weekend.

"Oh," said my daughter, "we had a wonderful time. We had a weekend of our simple joys."

"What?" I asked.

"Each of us wrote out a list of our simple joys, and then we each got to choose one to do alone and one to do together. We had a great weekend!" she answered.

"How do you define 'simple joys'?" I asked.

These were the criteria:

1. It has to be something you love to do.

2. It should not cost money—or very, very little.

3. It has to be something you can do within the area where you live or in your own home.

4. It can be accomplished within an hour or two.

5. It is something that you can do alone (this one is optional).

Suddenly in our family and among our friends one of our simple joys became making our list. My list started with doing the crossword puzzle in bed and went on to browsing in a bookstore, taking an early-morning walk, getting the first choice in a new box of chocolates, visiting an art museum, having an unexpected visitor, planning a party, standing in the wind . . . The list grew longer and longer. Just creating the list was a celebration of memories and happy thoughts.

On a recent wedding anniversary, my husband's work was so demanding that we could not travel anywhere. He surprised me, though, with taking the day off (which meant we could be together, the very best of all the joys in my life!) and we consulted our "simple joys" lists. We planned the entire day around our simple joys, and it was one of the most wonderful days of our lives.

A list of one's own simple joys is worth creating. It gives us a resource for unexpected empty moments; it gives us satisfaction and joy in times of poverty or sickness; it gives us a finer sense of who we are and what happiness is right at our fingertips; it helps rid us of the habits of purchased pleasures and frenetic fun.

In our busy lives, so often circumscribed by the man-made world of cement, walls, and electronic amusements, we need to be extremely careful to remind ourselves—and to teach our children— to observe the magnificence of the world around us, to genuinely and deeply appreciate the creations of the Lord. No child should be deprived of the wonders of nature or the zest and celebration of experiencing the elements.

The art of celebration builds into life the patterns of appreciating the natural earth. We should study the things that catch our attention or about which our children ask questions.

"How does a firefly light?" asked by a wondering child as he looks into the twilight should be an immediate impetus to go to the encyclopedia or to the library and experience the joy of finding out the splendid complexity of simple things.

Learning the specific names of plants is a marvelous and simple way for adults and children to enhance their delight in the beauties of the earth.

In California is a great ornamental plant that blooms in a sunburst—a ball of purple flowers exploding at the end of a long, slender stem. The plant is a member of the garlic family. Everyone is familiar with it, for it graces nearly every home, but it seems even more beautiful to those who know the name—"agapantha." Knowing the name gives a sense of ownership. The simple joy of the flower is made more joyful by the simple act of learning the name.

Other simple joys: clean sheets, getting a letter, sending a letter, certain dear voices, singing in the shower, a new fact, the smell of bread baking, the hot crust of a fresh loaf of bread, a telephone call made or received, a shiny clean floor, a new book, an anticipated film, a new nature walk, happy exhaustion at the end of a challenging day, an apple, an empty beach, a beloved spot on the earth revisited, a witty comment, laughter, rocking a child, listening to a child, seeing a child succeed at a task, comforting a child, birds in the morning, butterflies in the afternoon.

I urge you to make your own list of simple joys, following the criteria set down by my daughter and her husband or by setting your own dimensions of what you consider a simple joy to be. You will have a wonderful time thinking about it and adding to it.

Just creating the list will give you more joy than you can imagine, and it will help waken you to the continuing celebration of your life. Savor and celebrate.

If you want to be happy, be.

Leo Tolstoy, 1828–1910

5

....

I Did It My Way,
and I Am Getting
Better at It All the Time

*C*elebration is often a homemade product. It is
as personal as the individual, as original as the mind
that creates it, as happy as the boundaries of the heart
and spirit that feel it. When we choose to create events
of celebration they will grow out of our own individual talents, skills, desires, tastes, and concepts of
delight.

To one person a formal sit-down dinner may be the
ultimate expression of celebration. To another it may
be a camping trip or a rock-climbing expedition. The
goal for which one person may save with eager anticipation might be a mountain bike; for another, it might
be a piece of furniture or a university course.

Celebration is the bounteous feast of human experience, a table spread with wholesome, joyous, delightful, precious opportunities.

We get to make up our own plate.

Some of the ways and means of celebration I have discovered may give you some new thoughts about more celebratory experiences in the daily patterns of your own life. Some of these ideas may just sound like work or a waste of time. You may have a very different way of finding delight. It is not *how* you do it that matters—it is that you *do* do it. And actually, all these ideas take much more time to explain than they take to do. With most of them, the event is unchanged, just put in a different setting by a few moments of thought and effort. That is what celebration is all about.

My family has lived in seven states and twelve different communities. It has been important in the celebration of our lives to have a sense of resource and intellectual and emotional investment in the geographic area around us. We celebrate living in new areas by practicing the art of day-tripping. It is a wonderful way, wherever you live, to celebrate your own unique life.

Day-Trips

When we move to a new area, often with very unhappy and homesick children in tow and often with a homesick and unhappy heart of my own, the first thing I do is look for books on local history and local points of interest, and I study the books.

For a really great day-trip we do not go to big commercial attractions like amusement parks. All of our family have an aversion to crowds and standing in line.

There are many ways to hunt for a prime day-trip location. Some great day-trips might be to small towns where your ancestors or relatives might have settled. Ask friends and neighbors about interesting locations.

I found a great book on ghost towns in a bookstore. What a lot of great day-trips were in that book!

Always, always, always be searching for books and information about the area in which you live. Scour the library, bookstores, and your family history. Be prepared to stop at historic markers on the highway. When you see an interesting building, turn off your usual route and explore it. Ask questions, and read.

For example, on the outskirts of Park City, Utah, is a wonderful nineteenth-century farmhouse, now an inn. We passed the establishment year after year and then decided we had to know more. Our subsequent day-trip to Park City and dinner at Snowed Inn turned into a wonderful evening of food, conversation, and the story of a woman's memories of her grandparents' farm, which she had re-created on that piece of land.

What we like best in day-tripping is to find an unusual possibility—a town, or historic place, or natural region that we have never heard about before but that has enough information in the guide books to catch our attention.

Look for locally published books on day-trips. They usually have such titles as "Children's Outings around and about _____" or "Day-Trips in and around _____." Another good source of information is books titled "Walking Tours of _____." In New York, for example, we read in a small local pamphlet about the John Jay home (not exactly a household word or a tourist attraction but a *splendid* day-trip); in California, the town of Julian and the J. Paul Getty Museum (off-season); in Dallas, the towns of Jefferson, Mineral Wells, and Waxahachie (all with local guidebooks that told us what to look for); in Ohio, the nutting farms and chrysanthemum fields; and many, many more, too numerous to enumerate, almost too numerous to remember.

Here are some of the guidelines and policies we have adopted for successful day-tripping:

1. The most important part is to start with good information—an excellent guidebook and a detailed map. The more obscure the destination, the better we like it, because that lends an air of discovery to the enterprise and makes us feel a little proprietary toward the experience. We like the feeling of exploring, that there is a little element of chance in the whole day.

2. Individual reports from family members, if appropriate. For example, when we went to the San Diego Zoo, each child researched a different exotic animal and gave the report in the car as we drove down.

3. Clothes should be comfortable, clean, and attractive enough so that the family can enter any establishment without looking too inappropriate, but definitely casual enough to enjoy the car ride and physical activity.

4. The family should be prepared—and expect—to do a lot of walking. Take comfortable shoes and jackets in case of rain or a change in the weather.

5. Leave right on time.

We have numerous games we play in the car, as I am sure every family has. We play Twenty Questions, Just Suppose, singing games, Trivial Pursuit without the board, and so on. But mostly, on the way to a day trip, we spend the time talking about where we are going and what we hope to see and do. The history or importance of the place is discussed in some detail.

The reason we take no food or toys in the car is that they create a mess—and arguments. One of the most exciting events of the day will be discovering unusual and wonderful places to eat—a classic diner, home-made pies, a hundred-year-old inn, a tiny Mexican house in Old Town, a sandwich and soup shop on the main street run by two spinster sisters—just wonderful places. That is our one financial investment in the experience.

6. For good day-tripping, the place should not be farther than an hour and a half's drive—if it is something *really* wonderful, two hours might be allowed, but that is the absolute limit of driving time for a successful day.

Your research has given you some idea of what you want to see, but the important part of day-tripping is the unexpected. Be as flexible as you can. If you see a sign by the side of the road—like the sign on I-15 in the desert between Los Angeles and Las Vegas that says, "Calico Ghost Town—Five Miles," with an arrow that points to a narrow road leading straight across the empty desert toward some barren, rocky mountains on the distant horizon—well, turn off the road and bounce across the desert!

We did just that—turned off the road, bumped across the barren desert, and discovered an abandoned ghost town, now being restored. The day we went there only ten or twelve other people were walking the hot, dusty main street.

The children bought penny candy in the old general store, rode the cog railroad, saw an abandoned mine, and learned the remarkable story of Lucy, who had lived alone in the last standing house on the main street when the town was otherwise completely deserted. She had lived there until she died. No grass, no trees, no shrubs—just the bare shacks and the one street baking in the sun.

7. Be friendly and ask questions. We have discovered wonderful things by simply striking up conversations with people who live in the place we are visiting. When we visited Mineral Wells, Texas, we tramped through the deserted lobby of the old Baker Hotel. It was a haunting experience. The huge old resort was closed in preparation for being torn down. In its empty rooms we heard the echoes of hundreds of past experiences—dances, banquets, Hollywood stars, wealthy families who had vacationed in those cavernous rooms, bathed in the sulphur springs, and been pampered in the glamorous spa. We were the only ones in the building, and the old caretaker showed us through the enormous dining halls, lobbies, gymnasium, theater (where Mary Martin made her debut). It was a most remarkable experience.

As we left, the caretaker said, "You ought to go see the old dude ranch, too." What dude ranch? we asked, because there was nothing about it in our guidebook. He gave us directions, and the day became one of such unusual experience that it is hard to describe. We drove through the Texas countryside toward the Brazos River, and, following his detailed directions, we turned on country road after country road through cactus, cattle fields, and mesquite until, making a last turn by a stand of dusty live oak, we saw two stone pillars and a large, curved iron sign that said simply, "Dude Ranch." The sign was red with rust and looked about to collapse.

After entering through the gate we drove down a road that had once been graveled but was now just dust. On either side were the remnants of oleander and laurel, long since run wild and withering in the heat. At one time it must have been a beautiful drive.

We found the ranch. It was a low, Spanish-style brick building, square, with a courtyard, and an old tiled swimming pool that was green with moss. Beyond the residence was a huge empty stable, a rodeo ring with bleachers, and a race track oval overgrown with prairie grass—all going to ruin.

The proprietor, an old, gnarled, sunburned man, happily showed us into the main lobby—a long, once-beautiful room with windows overlooking the slope to the river and a stone fireplace at one end. The room was dimly lit because the windows were thick with dirt, and the space—from wall to wall—was crammed with dust-covered antiques, mostly large armoires, china cabinets, and bulky buffets. It was impossible to walk between them. Chairs and tables and old sofas were stacked one upon the other.

"We were in the antique business for a while after the dude ranch business began to decline. We keep meaning to ship this stuff off to a dealer somewhere but just haven't found the time," the elderly man told us. Some of the pieces, collecting dust, the wood drying out from lack of care, were absolutely beautiful.

He showed us walls of pictures of people who had been guests at the ranch in its heyday: Cary Grant, Clark Gable, Lucille Ball, Desi Arnaz—almost any significant actor or actress of the 1950s and 60s. In the pictures, which showed the beauty of the establishment when it was thriving, was a handsome, tall man in his mid years, wearing riding clothes and standing by a splendid palomino. The owner grinned as we looked at the picture. "Yes," he said, "that's me."

We looked at the old man carefully, but, just as we could see only a shadow of the former magnificence of the ranch, so we could hardly glimpse that handsome, vigorous, prosperous young horseman in this bent, weathered, aged man. How swiftly life sweeps on.

Before we left, the kind and lonely man took us through a stand of shrub oak, pine, and mesquite to another location. "This was our dance hall and recreational building," he said wistfully. "It burned down about fifteen years ago, and we've never seemed to get around to rebuilding it."

We saw the outline of a lovely building. Mexican tile, some of it in mint condition, paved what had once been the floor, and we saw the remnants of a tall, field-rock chimney and stone steps. Broken window frames clung to the remnant of a burned wall. Ivy and creeping oak were growing in the cracks, and vines were obscuring the foundation.

It must have been such a lovely place on a warm Texas night, filled with glamorous people, the orchestra playing, and the river sparkling in the moonlight. Now it was like seeing a dream.

Our children scrambled down the banks of the river and threw rocks in the swift waters, and then, mulling over what we had seen—amazed, as though we had been wafted into some other place and time—we returned to the car and drove home. A perfect day-trip!

8. Have physical exertion. As our children grew older and our boys wanted more physical adventure, we chose other kinds of day-trips. When we went to Jefferson, Texas, we arranged for a canoe trip in the afternoon. Often a hike or a bike ride—or horseback riding—will give that physical exertion which is a necessary part of day-tripping. And, always do as much

walking as possible—you see more and experience more that way.

I will never forget the day-trip to Solvang, California, when our college sons and their friends rode the bicycle buggies that are the mode of transportation in downtown Solvang. They are like two tandem bicycles joined together by seats with a striped awning over them. They are meant to be a very genteel mode of locomotion. Well, these young men saw different possibilities in them, and so they pumped their way to a side street and then began a wild race.

It got funnier and funnier as people gathered to watch these eight young men, pedaling as though demons were after them, perspiration drenching their faces, and the striped awnings flapping as they had never flapped before. It was one of the best afternoons ever.

A bicycle buggy race in staid Solvang! What a celebration!

Day-trips are an inexpensive way of traveling, learning history, seeing museums, enjoying family, having recreation—and growing to love and feel connected to the place in which you live.

Making Family a Celebration

I was a dinner guest at a young family's home. Next to their dining table was an open area of tiled floor on which there was no furniture. I soon understood why.

After the meal was over, the children went over to the stereo, which sits on a counter in that area, and put in a tape. It was classical music with a strong, colorful rhythm and melody that set the fingers tapping. In an instant all of the children were dancing. It was such fun! The boys were leaping and doing "boy" stuff, and the girls were pirouetting and jumping. It was beautiful and amazingly fun. Dancing after supper. Instant celebration.

To create recipes for delight is one of our great privileges as homemakers, as friends, as mothers and grandmothers.

Changing the ordinary into a celebration often requires just one thought. Just one simple idea. Just a fraction of imagination and effort. Fourteen of my grandchildren were coming over for the afternoon. I had already planned the activity: we were going to the arboretum to see the spring flower show, the biggest display of tulips in the state. I knew, however, that some of the older children would be less than excited when they heard our destination, and not one of the children was going to want to get back into the van and drive another half hour as soon as they arrived.

So . . . I came up with a celebration plan. I was going to take them on a "World Tour." I quickly got out paper and drew a map for each child. We were going to Mexico, Holland, and France!

Our first stop was "Mexico" (Taco Bell), and while we drove there we sang Mexican songs and tried to think of everything we knew about that country.

Another trick I have learned about having fun is to *limit the time.* When we go to a museum or a restaurant or a place where I feel the children need to have an added impetus to their fun, I set a time limit that makes the seeing, or doing, very tight. They have to hurry to get everything in, so finishing within the time limit becomes a challenge—and challenges are fun.

We had twenty minutes to order and eat, and then, all wearing the Mexican hats that were the gift of the restaurant, we hurried back into the van. (Getting into the car can also be timed and a prize given to those who get into the seat belts on time, turning a part of the day that is a chore into a game.)

"Holland" was next. The tulips at the arboretum were magnificent. The weather was perfect. The children ran in the open air, in the midst of complete and utter beauty. We divided into teams, and each team had to gather three new facts to share in the car when we met later.

The older boys had not expected to enjoy it, but the fresh air, the garden spreading before us, the old mansion, the lake—all worked their magic even on the boys, who found themselves eagerly and competitively becoming experts on tulips, hyacinths, jonquils, and forsythia.

Tired, excited, we left "Holland," and drove to "France," a French bakery near my home where everyone got to choose a pastry and eat it at the sidewalk tables. We talked about trying to decide what famous person we would like to have come down the sidewalk, and I taught them French words for several common objects.

Nothing was different about that day—I had simply done the activities I had planned—but putting them into the context of world travel made the children feel they had visited remarkable and extraordinary places. It made all the difference in making a splendid and special day. A fairly ordinary day became a real celebration.

Many of the same techniques work with adults. Several of our grown, married children were visiting, and we decided to see *Much Ado about Nothing*. It was just a movie, but I wanted to make the day one of celebration. We began the evening before with a menu of English food, and then we reviewed the plot of *Much*

Ado and read portions of the play with different members of the family taking parts.

We planned, after the movie, to attend a medieval fair, but it was raining heavily and the fair was canceled. Nevertheless, the movie was spectacular—and especially wonderful to us because the night before we had reviewed the plot line and the characters.

At the end of the movie, wonder of wonders, the lights came on and the three rows of people in front of us stood up. They were all dressed in Elizabethan costume. Amazing! We learned they were the cast from the Medieval Fair. When it was rained out, they had decided to go to the movie.

What a great finale! We talked and laughed—and then, we went over to Pier One, where everybody purchased one item that reminded them of the evening. Forsooth! It was a grand time.

Making Ordinary Occasions Wonderful

Names. I have discovered that naming something gives it more delight—naming is a form of celebration in and of itself. It can be a very simple name. "The Nutcracker Night," for example, was the name I gave to an evening of celebration for my grandchildren. Christmas was coming, and the *Nutcracker* ballet was to be performed on television. I knew from long experience that the children might well become bored with the ballet, so I determined I would make it a night to remember.

First I gave it its name. Then, using that name, I told the children to find costumes for the evening show. They could dress like any of the characters in the ballet—and so, before they put together their costumes, I read them the story. As they were upstairs conspiring, going through closets, raiding the cupboards and linen shelves, I prepared a "Russian" supper. Actually, it was just cream of corn soup with meatballs and toasted rye bread. It was such an odd combination of foods that they were certain what they were eating was foreign.

For dessert we had "Russian Snowballs" (again, I gave the dessert a name, but it was really just ice cream rolled in coconut with chocolate sauce).

At each commercial break during the show we talked about what was happening in the ballet, and, during the ensemble scenes, all of the children got up and danced with the corps de ballet. It was a glorious "Nutcracker Night." The magic of celebration is that the one doing the planning and other work has as much fun as the participants.

Costumes. There is something about even the suggestion of a costume that marks an event as a celebration. When one daughter returned from her mission in Montreal, I wanted to have an evening of celebration. I found a charming French restaurant a short distance from our home, but I wanted to do something more, something to make it unique. I thought of Montreal and how chic the women are there, and so I decided it would be "hats." All my daughters and daughters-in-law who were going to be at the dinner came with me to an inexpensive store that carried hats. We tried on hats to our heart's content, and finally each of us chose one.

That night we sailed into the restaurant looking quite wonderful, a little conspicuous, and very, very festive. We had the most splendid time, and I always think of that evening with a thrill of delight at the memory of all those beautiful, beloved faces set off by their elegant hats.

But first a song. Books, art, and music are essential

components of celebration. We have always sung as a family, and it has delighted us to see, as our children marry, how quickly they teach the extensive list of our family songs to their partners. We especially love rounds and have made quite a collection of them. Some of our favorites are "My Dame Has a Lame Tame Crane," "Chairs to Mend," "Buy, Buy, Buy," and "Black Socks."

Work. Work is the ultimate game. Our favorite method of turning work into a party is with a bowl in the kitchen. In the bowl are placed slips of paper, each listing one of the Saturday chores. Also in the bowl are several slips describing unusual tasks, such as "go around the house and tell every person something nice about himself," or "get a cookie out of the cupboard, pour a glass of milk or juice, sit down, and enjoy yourself for five minutes," or "run the circumference of the house three times singing 'Yankee Doodle Dandy.'" Those are the fun slips. If you draw a job slip, you just go do the job, but if you draw a fun slip, then you do it and place the fun slip back in the bowl. You may not do two fun slips in a row but must keep drawing until you get a job slip.

There are many ways to make work a game. And work, when it is finished, is sheer delight.

Other ideas to make the ordinary into extraordinary are notes, decorations, candles, ribbons, written menus, homemade tickets, eating in different places in the house, surprises, unexpected gifts, bubble-blowing, contests, challenges, and treats or notes placed on plates or pillows or in lunch boxes. Just add the unexpected to the expected.

Sports and Games

We can incorporate into our daily lives sports,

games, and the lively arts. They are the bright, satin ribbons that highlight the threads of life we are weaving.

We all need physical activity to whet the keenness of our ability to enjoy celebration, and many games can become the center of celebration: tennis round-robin, Ping-Pong, touch football, soccer, dodgeball, swimming, mountain climbing, volleyball, playing in the local park. Physical activity may yield great joy.

Table games and word games can create moments of celebration. We love games, especially word games and games of wit. One son-in-law has a Monopoly board he has had since he was a boy. Each game he plays is recorded on the board—the date, who played, and who won. With that simple tradition he has made playing Monopoly a celebration.

Traditions

Traditions are an important part of the celebrations of our lives. The repetition of things we love leaves deep and happy impressions in our minds and spirits and helps us to live with rejoicing.

For several years I made sweatshirts for every member of the family to wear at Thanksgiving. (Thanksgiving is my favorite celebration! To me, Christmas is the carols, the being together, and the renewal of my relationship with the Savior. My big focus on *doing* is at Thanksgiving.)

Each year I chose a different theme and then used it in the table decorations as well. One year it was ducks; another, it was apples; another, home; another, quilts; and so on.

I did not decorate the men's sweatshirts, except with a little monogram on the sleeve, but we all had a shirt of the same color—from the biggest man to the smallest baby—to wear on the hike that is a traditional part of our Thanksgiving celebration.

Now, lest you be overwhelmed by the thought of my decorating all those sweatshirts, you should know that I did it with lots of help from my daughters, and I didn't do the shirts with anything like meticulous perfection. Once I even spray-painted them (talk about a quickie method!) with stencils.

When it stopped being fun and became a chore, I stopped making the shirts. I don't believe in tradition running away with joy—and so, the year that I sighed at the thought of all the work to make them, I just cancelled the sweatshirts. The family has the memory of the sweatshirts and the pictures—and good memories are a very nice part of celebration.

Probably no traditions are filled with more precious warmth than those of Christmas. Each family's Christmas traditions are perhaps the greatest expression of celebration.

One caution: when an event becomes so crusted with traditions that we find ourselves dreading the work rather than eagerly looking forward to the event, when the doing is no longer a delight, then we are serving the tradition—the tradition is no longer serving us. When those feelings occur, remember the principle of simplification and restore the things that matter so that the celebration will be untarnished and bright once again.

Funquik

It's hard to create celebration on the spur of the moment without some raw materials on hand. I call these supplies Funquik, and I like to have them on my shelves at all times. What might alert you that you need your Funquik box? (Your Funquik box should always be kept in its Funquik place, to which no one has access but you.)

Here are some of the clues that your Funquik box is needed: children are bored or quarreling, you are feeling sorry for yourself, the children are restless and cranky, you feel you have no money and no time to do something fun, you're resentful at being cooped up at home, or you feel like this day is just another in a long line of same-old-thing days.

When you are having these feelings, it is time to take control of what is happening. A Funquik box and a little imagination can create a project or a new experience or a quiet hour for the children while you can do something you want to do.

Some of the things in my Funquik box are writing paper, construction paper, pencils, marker pens, paints, tape, scissors, glue, glitter, ribbons, balls and paddles, music and video tapes, inexpensive gifts, felt, scraps, old magazines, and so on. The children use duplicates of some of these items all the time. The ones in my Funquik box are used only under my supervision—when I get the box out.

If there are no children in your life, your Funquik box may hold a new book you want to read, or a crossword puzzle, or an envelope for saving dollar bills toward a day on the ski slopes—you get the picture.

With a Funquik box and a little imagination, the fuse of celebration can be relit. The real secret of celebration is that it is usually just one idea away.

To see a World in a Grain of Sand
And a Heaven in a Wild Flower,
Hold Infinity in the palm of your hand
And Eternity in an hour.

William Blake, 1757–1827

6

··

The Glory of God
Is Intelligence

*B*ooks! The very word makes me shiver with wonder and delight. I was reared in a home where books and the gift of words were cherished. We had a dictionary next to our dining room table so that we could look up words because, as we were growing up, we frequently had heated discussions about the specific meaning of words.

My brothers, my sister, and I, as well as our parents, were constant readers. By every chair, bed, and resting place a book or magazine lay open. We talked and argued and shared—conversation was often centered on what we were reading.

The love of words was planted early, and now, in my mature years, I revel in the harvest of those early influences. My brothers—two scientists, a lawyer, and an economist—are all poets of merit, and my sister teaches creative writing at Arizona State University. The greatest inheritance our parents gave us was the love of books and learning.

Knowledge is the fundamental fuel of thought. Confucius said that learning without thought is labor lost but thought without learning is a perilous enterprise. As we read Doctrine and Covenants 93 we are taught the interrelationship between truth, knowledge, intelligence, and the glory of God. Wisdom, or intelligence, is described as light and truth. Light refers to the enlightenment of the spirit through the Holy Ghost, the scriptures, the inspiration of the Lord, and the light of Christ. Truth is "knowledge of things as they are, as they were, and as they are to come." This knowledge, combined with prayer, pondering, and spiritual light, becomes a lifetime pursuit of exaltation—the ultimate celebration.

Joseph Smith has told us that we are saved no faster than we get knowledge (*Teachings of the Prophet Joseph Smith,* sel. Joseph Fielding Smith [Salt Lake City: Deseret Book, 1938], p. 217). The ability to comprehend, to become enlightened, is a gift from the Lord, but he expects us to study, search, think, and learn throughout our lives so that we comprehend the things he would teach us. We are encouraged to study all things in heaven and earth, things above the earth and under the earth. We are to study out of the best books and to learn of other peoples and languages, even unto the isles of the sea.

It is the true celebration of mortal life to be endlessly curious about everything, to know and understand, as Doctrine and Covenants 93 explains, all truth and intelligence, which is "independent in the sphere in which God has placed it" (v. 30). We have been given our agency to receive this truth and light, but it must be by our own agency, or effort. If we refuse to study and learn when we have the opportunity, then in that failure to gain knowledge, the scriptures say, we are condemned.

We stand on an earth that seems solid to us, yet the matter that we take for granted is in constant motion. Each atom is filled with motion, crystals are moving slowly and inexorably toward formation, the earth itself is rotating and swinging in majestic orbit—the whole of space is filled with motion. We do not even begin to comprehend the things that lie about us in full sight.

Discovery, says the scientist Albert Gyorgie, consists of seeing what everybody has seen and thinking what nobody has thought. What a perfect description of truth mixed with light which results in eternal intelligence—or the glory of God.

As parents we teach the eternal quest for knowledge both by precept and by example. Reading should be as much a part of our lives as washing our face and hands. We should read to ourselves, and we should read to our children and grandchildren.

We live in a world that is in jeopardy of losing the gift of language. Our children are more computer literate than word literate. Publications have lowered their vocabulary and sentence structure—their readability levels—significantly, to high school level or below.

The ability to read well, indeed, the ability to read at all, is being compromised in our culture. Even those with educations often feel that the day they receive their diploma is the end of their years of study. Many well-educated men and women simply do not consider the acquisition of further knowledge a continuing part of life's experience. I contrast such stagnant attitudes with that of my mother, who, in her eighties took a course in anthropology because she wondered about the migrations of the "family of man."

In the continuing ability to feel wonder and curiosity—in the hunger and thirst that comes from awareness and the need to know—comes the lifelong motivation to study and learn. Seeking to gain knowledge is both the badge of the celebrating heart and the nourishment of renewed celebration. It should last as long as breath.

Knowledge is a great, self-starting pursuit—it perpetuates itself. Each little bit of knowledge we gain leads us to more questions, more desire to know. Gaining knowledge is not only the pursuit of glory, it is also the glorious pursuit. The search for knowledge and learning is not ended with a graduation from formal institutions of learning. That is just the beginning.

There are many aspects to the lifelong pursuit of knowledge. Part of knowledge is certainly the development of our talents.

My brother commented to a seminary class, "All of you have your agency. It is an absolute gift. The Lord has put no limitations upon your agency—but you have put limitations on it. For example, all of you are completely free to walk up to the front of this class and play a Bach prelude. You have the agency to do so and the piano is here. Most of you, however, are not able to do so. Your ability to exercise that agency will exist only when you have spent years studying, practicing, and learning to play."

When we understand the implications of that statement, we understand that our own lack of effort and knowledge inhibits our agency in many of the things we might wish to do.

Knowledge is gained in many ways: experience;

experiments; careful observation; lessons, discussions and lectures; meditation and prayer; effort and practice. All of these are important skills to be used in gaining knowledge.

Books—the fruit of other people's learning—form the background of our own learning. In books and other writings can be gathered the total of all that is known upon this earth.

Books also contain the lovely creations of humankind, the epic poetry and other beautifully crafted thoughts. I will never forget the day in autumn when I walked across the sunlit campus at Brigham Young University toward the Quonset huts that ringed the campus in the fifties. It was late afternoon, and the sidewalk was deserted. My destination was a small graduate class in Greek literature taught by Dr. Hugh B. Nibley. Handsome, youthful, and brilliant, Dr. Nibley was already a legend on the campus.

Only four or five other students sat with me in the hot metal building. Ten minutes passed, and the young man next to me said, "Ten minutes past class time. We don't have to wait any longer. I'm outta here!" He started picking up his books, and the rest of us looked uncertain.

At that moment the back door banged open, and we heard footsteps running up the aisle. We turned to see Dr. Nibley. He was wearing an old army sweater, his pant cuff was wrapped in a bicycle clip, and his hair was blowing in the wind of his motion. In his arms he carried two huge leather volumes which he slammed onto the lecture table. He turned to greet us in his eager voice. Speaking at breathtaking speed, he walked back and forth in front of us, his eyes sparking with excitement.

"What would you *do*," he exclaimed delightedly, "if I told you that they have just discovered a machine that will allow you to live in the mind of a man who lived three thousand years ago?

"I mean," he went on, his voice so swift, intense, and exuberant that I felt breathless just listening, "I mean, not just look at his brain. No! Literally be in his mind! Hear what he hears! Think what he thinks! Smell what he smells! Feel what he feels!?"

He paused and looked at us intensely for a moment. Then he went over and picked up one of the heavy volumes, and he shook it in our faces.

"Well!" he said with a triumphant smile and a voice of great celebration. "Surprise, surprise! Here it is! Here it is!"

I looked up at the book looming over my head, and I felt the fire of his conviction.

Of course! Through the wonder of books for a time we can experience and think great thoughts, great events, great ideas. Through books, in one lifetime we can live a thousand lives!

One precious thing that reading will do for us besides increasing our knowledge is give us comfort in times of trial. Reading gives us the opportunity to escape briefly from the turmoil and challenge of our own lives and to return to them refreshed and wiser. Reading can amuse, enlighten, reassure, teach, and enlarge our understanding.

All true knowledge begins and ends in the study of the scriptures. If we are to have lives of celebration, we must build each day upon the words of the Lord. In each life the reading of the scriptures will take a different form. The important thing is that it be constant and real. My husband has read daily for more than twenty-five years without missing a single day. He reads a chapter of the Book of Mormon each morning and a chapter of one of the other books of scripture each evening. Each time he completes the Book of Mormon, he marks the date in the front of his book.

I am a student of the scriptures, too, but my reading tends to be lesson oriented—or manuscript oriented. Often when I am reading I will begin a train of thought and end up pursuing it through assorted scriptures. And some days I just plain miss reading altogether.

I was determined to follow my husband's disciplined example, and so, the last time he began reading the Book of Mormon, I began with him on the same day. "This way,"I said optimistically, "we can discuss the chapter at the end of the day."

Shortly afterwards, Weston began an intensive period of traveling, and I was called to be Young Women president. Several weeks went by, and our joint reading project was not discussed.

One night, after returning home from a long business trip, Weston said sleepily, "I just read Alma 17. Where are you reading?"

I was still in Mosiah, but I did not want to admit it. I smiled. "If you keep reading at your present rate you'll catch up to me before you know it—the second time around!" We both went to sleep laughing. The next day I started reading at Alma 17. After all, knowledge is patient, and it doesn't have deadlines except in school.

As we study the scriptures it becomes very clear that Heavenly Father desires that we search for knowledge throughout out lives. When I say knowledge, I mean truth plus the Light of Christ—or in other words, wisdom or intelligence, not intellectualism. Intellectualism is referred to in the scriptures as "learning" or "learned," and it is depicted as a deterrent to spiritual growth.

It is important to understand the difference between knowledge, which creates joy and growth, and intellectualism, which destroys the spirit.

Here are some guidelines to help distinguish between intellectualism and knowledge:

Knowledge never builds barriers between us and others. It creates a deep understanding of others and asserts the common ties that bind all of mankind.

Intellectualism considers itself superior to others.

Knowledge gives us vision and supports and reinforces spiritual truth. It helps us to see the mark that we must not miss or see beyond. It teaches us the sublime simplicities.

Intellectualism deliberately obfuscates (and uses words like that!) and delights in obscure complication rather than clarification.

Knowledge ponders and is obedient. The knowledgeable mind does not fear wise direction and does not insist on its point of view.

Intellectualism defies direction and desires constant rethinking, believing nothing is constant.

Knowledge teaches how much we have yet to learn. It teaches us the value of the Spirit and the ideas of others regardless of their education. Knowledge makes us truly humble.

Intellectualism makes us proud and causes us to jealously guard what we know to use against others to convince, control, or win. It causes us to have faith in the learning of man rather than in the Spirit of the Lord.

Finally, true knowledge fills the countenance with truth and light and makes us more approachable, open, and understanding—more loving. Joseph Smith spent his life seeking knowledge and gained it, yet it only made him more loving and beloved.

The mark of godlike intelligence on the face of a man or a woman is truly the most appealing and moving expression that one can see. To wear such a face would be a celebration.

I wish to spread the doctrine of the strenuous life.

Theodore Roosevelt, 1859–1919

7

···

Be There

*A*t the end of the movie *Forrest Gump*, the main character, a simple and ingenuous man, accompanies his young son to the bus stop. The little boy is going to his first day of school, and his father watches with concern, pride, and love as the child climbs onto the school bus. "I'll be here when you come home," Forrest calls to his son as the bus door closes. The bus drives away, and Forrest sits down on a stump.

Suddenly it dawns on the audience that the father will sit there all day. The first thing his son will see when he returns that afternoon will be his beloved father in the same spot, waiting for him. The camera pulls back, and a pure white feather, wafted on the tender breezes, slowly drifts toward Forrest, as he sits quietly and faithfully at his post. The feather brushes against him like some great beneficence, a blessing, a mark of approval drifting from heaven.

Celebration can be as humble as quiet, unadorned faithfulness. There is great celebration in the knowledge that we are where we should be when we should be there. Celebration exists in our determination to acknowledge the times when our attendance—just being there—is the measure of who and what we are and our willingness to put first things first in our lives.

My father taught me this principle of celebration. He taught me that we have an invitation from the Lord and we, His children, should answer it continually.

A parable describes a banquet planned by the Master. He invites his friends—noblemen, prominent and important people. When the time for the feast comes, not one invited guest is there. The invitation is then rescinded. It is now too late for those who were first invited, and others, who are humbler, more obedient and open to his voice, are asked to take their places at the table.

This parable is often overlooked, yet it contains an invaluable message for those of us who have been invited to the banquet—who have heard the invitation, have been baptized, and have become, by our own promises, friends of the Master who will be there, but then we begin to fail to appreciate the invitation unless we receive some special recognition or responsibility— just having been invited is no longer enough for us.

During the past two decades, I have noticed a dramatic change in attitudes toward attendance at meetings, activities, and a large array of events. "I'm too busy," or "I don't attend ward parties—they are never much fun," or "My children can't go to weekday Mutual activities because they have so much homework and other important things to do," or "Homemaking meeting is not my thing."

My father was a bishop for many years, and when he was released he was without a calling for a while. I know it was difficult for him to have been the leader of the ward and then suddenly be "without portfolio."

One Sunday morning, very early, I went down to the library in our home to practice the hymns I was going to accompany in Sunday School that day, and I found my father, dressed in his suit and fresh white shirt with his crisp pocket handkerchief, sitting in his chair, reading the Sunday School manual.

"Are you teaching Sunday School class today?" I asked.

"No," said my father, "but I am going to be a student in it."

"Do you always read the lesson, even when you are not teaching it?" I asked, dumbfounded. "When you don't even have a calling?"

"Jaroldeen," he said gravely, "I have a sacred calling. I am a member of The Church of Jesus Christ, and just being a member entails life-filling responsibilities. Like any other calling, I want to do this one well. My responsibility is to attend every meeting and listen and contribute to the best of my ability. I must be friendly and cordial to all who are there. I must study and read the scriptures so that I bring the Spirit of the Lord with me. I must do my home teaching, encourage the bishop and other officers, care for my family and set them an example of faithfulness, and search for opportunities to serve others."

He smiled and repeated, "Just being a member is a challenging job!"

One great lesson of celebration is recognizing the challenge and joy of membership in the human race. Our lives do not have to contain any more recognition than that we *are* for them to be full of great opportunities.

We soon discover that if we are not in the places where we should be, when we should be there, we have diminished our ability to feel joy. A vague sense of guilt will nag at us, and even the most brilliant rationalization will be unable to rid us of the feeling of knowing we are not in the place we should be.

It is easy and fun to fulfill responsibilities, to attend meetings and events when we are in charge, or have control, or are in a visible role, but it is equally essential that we fulfill our responsibilities when our role is nothing more or less than to be there.

Life gets a lot easier, and more fun, when we make this principle of supportive attendance a policy. We don't have to evaluate whether to go or not to go, and we don't have to try to decide what will be worthwhile to us and what won't be.

The truth is, we do not know beforehand what the valuable part of an experience will be. It may not be the speaker, it may not be the activity, but it may be the making of a new friend, the encouragement of a leader, a word said to a downcast acquaintance, or just the opportunity to feel the satisfaction of having supported those to whom we owe our support.

Sometimes genuine conflicts make attendance impossible. Especially when we have a number of children, or our husband has a time-consuming career, we find that travel, school engagements, and community responsibilities will be scheduled at the same time as Church events or family obligations. In such cases we must evaluate which is most essential. Such choices are inevitable and will be made on their own merits. Nevertheless, we must be sure our priorities are right.

The policy of the joyful, celebratory life is that if we belong, we, to the best of our ability, will be in attendance at the scheduled meetings of the Church, PTA, choir, and volunteer organizations, and at weddings, funerals, birthdays, children's programs and other family events, showers, elections, and all the other obligations our life entails. Being a faithful member is a wonderful experience.

Once we have adopted this policy, it is amazing the freedom and satisfaction it brings. No longer do we have to excuse our absences to ourselves or anyone else. No longer do we have to try to evaluate the importance of individual events. No longer do we have to be the self-appointed judge of what is worthy of our attendance and what is not. And the shadow of guilt is a thing of the past.

The concept of not enough time is not often applicable. Just think, if someone invited you to a Barbra Streisand concert, you would probably find the time. When you give up the hour or two a month it takes to attend Homemaking, you simply get up earlier that day, or work harder, or stay up later if you need to. In truth, most of us take off a night or so a month anyway.

Our teenagers can also find ways in their week's schedules to make time for the hour they spend at Mutual. It isn't what they do at Mutual that matters. Don't try to weigh the value of attendance by weighing the activity against other possible uses of the time. The purpose of their regular attendance is develop the lifetime gift of being there where they should be, when they should be. Attendance becomes the measure of commitment and will be part of the iron rod of their life. They are also setting an example and making life-long relationships.

If we say that our teenager finds it more important to do schoolwork than to attend his scheduled activity, we ignore the fact that all the youth have schoolwork to do! If everyone used that excuse, we would lose our youth program altogether. If we say the youth program is doing unimportant things—that it would be better for our teenager to spend time practicing a musical instrument or sport—we are doing three things:

1. We are giving the unsaid message to our children that they are better, more gifted and exceptional than those who regularly support the program.

2. We are teaching our children that Church events are way down the ladder of value in their lives, that any obligation comes before supporting Church events, that they have the license to evaluate the quality of the event and, if it does not meet their standards, they are not expected to attend.

3. We give the strong message that if we live a busy life, we do not need to sacrifice to serve the Lord. Young men and women who as teenagers are told that they can be too busy to attend youth activities will become adults who as professionals or mothers will be too busy to say yes to being Relief Society president or Scoutmaster or Laurel leader.

The concept of being there means that we are promise-keepers and willing to be followers and supporters. It is the assurance that we will take a position and stay with it when others fall away. People such as this are those who, "while their companions slept, / Were toiling upward in the night" (Henry Wadsworth Longfellow, *The Ladder of Saint Augustine*). They are where they should be, first and last. They are the lamp-lit virgins at the midnight hour.

When my family and I were living in Connecticut, my husband was in a serious automobile accident. I ran to my neighbor, asked her to watch my little girl, and dashed to the hospital. I arrived at the hospital to find my neighbor's husband—a man I knew only slightly—

in the waiting room. He worked for a large corporation and he was preparing for an international trip, but the minute his wife called, he walked out of his office and drove to the hospital. "I am here, Jaroldeen," he said. "Is there anything you need? Anything we can do?" He did not telephone. He was simply there.

Another time, I was proofreading a large manuscript of more than six hundred pages. My New York publisher had given me only one week to return the proofs because we were on a very tight production schedule. I was Young Women president and had a week of several activities. As I was cleaning up Wednesday night after a Laurel dinner, I mentioned to two of my friends who worked in the youth program with me that I was afraid I was going to be unable to meet the deadline on my manuscript.

The next morning my doorbell rang. My two precious friends were there. They did not just call and say "Can we help?" They were there.

The three of us worked side by side, and the manuscript was in the mail by evening.

Being there is a principle of celebration because it causes us to move away from the limited scope of what we see and what we wish and what we focus on. To be there we are compelled into the world of others' needs and of obedience and sacrifice.

We can get so caught up in the overwhelming wonder and responsibility of our own life that we forget that our life, to have real value, must be lost in the lives of others. I love the story of the Lady of Shalott as she weaves her beautiful fabric and spends her days staring in the mirror. How many of us, if we were not compelled by the knowledge of our obligation to be there (not just in the places we want to be but also in the places we have promised to be or that we should be), would live our lives like Alfred, Lord Tennyson's beautiful, aloof, and empty lady, weaving the fabric of our own lives, seeing only ourselves and our own needs, doing only the things we want to do.

A few months ago I discussed the principle of being there in the Saturday session of stake conference. I said, "Stop asking yourself, Should I go? Is it going to be worth my while? or telling yourself, No one will miss me this once. Just be there," I said, "and you will be amazed at how simple it is to do it and what wonderful things can happen."

Sunday afternoon, I received a phone call from a dear young woman whom I visit teach. Her husband is investigating the Church, and she has two lively boys. That morning, she told me, her husband had decided not to attend the meeting, and she found herself thinking, "No one will know if I'm there. It is such a hassle with the boys. It won't matter this once."

"Then," she recounted, "I remembered what you had said, so I repeated to myself, 'Be there,' and the boys and I went. We got seats at the very back of the cultural hall, and I was sitting there thinking this wasn't such a good idea after all when a man walked past me, and I gasped with recognition. "I reached out and touched the man's arm. 'Are you David Jones [not his real name]?' I asked. He said yes." He was the former husband of her aunt, her favorite uncle when she was a child. The last time she had seen him, she was eleven years old.

Her uncle had not been a member of the Church when she knew him, and his marriage had broken up years before. She had wondered for more than a decade what had happened to him. "What are you doing here?" my friend asked him in amazement. She was thrilled to learn that since the divorce her uncle had investigated the Church, had been baptized, had remarried, and lived not far away.

She concluded tearfully, "He was such a wonderful part of my childhood, and our family had completely lost track of him. I came home filled with wonder. It was as though the Lord had said to me, "Be there—you never know what wonders I will perform."

Have you ever wondered about the people who didn't accept King Benjamin's invitation to hear him speak? "It's going to be so crowded," "I hate spending time in a tent," "Someone else can tell us what he said," "I'll wait and read the conference issue." Think what they missed!

What must it have been like to stand in that mighty congregation in Zarahemla and have the joy of feeling your heart undergo the mighty change? To be given the name of Christ as your own—to be blessed by the king whose life had been given to service?

No one could have imagined beforehand all that was going to happen. Those who attended did not go because they had foreknowledge that it would be a life-changing experience. They attended because they were covenant-keepers and King Benjamin's address unexpectedly became the watershed experience of their lives.

We feel that same satisfaction whenever we are in the right place at the right time. I love those events that reaffirm that just being—and being where we should be—gives our life affirmation and joy. Being there is such a simple, abiding celebration of the shared needs of humankind.

Being there is our quiet celebration—the gentle feather of joy that will brush against us as we sit quietly, just being a member.

To business that we love we rise betime,
And go to 't with delight.

William Shakespeare, 1564–1616

8

....

The Just-Can't-Wait
Principle

A phrase in the scriptures that I love is "joy
in the morning." When we lie down at night, before
sleep invades our consciousness, often the cares, fears,
and concerns of our life overwhelm us. It is as though,
in the darkness, all the worries we have held at bay
during the busy hours of the day suddenly come rush-
ing over us.

What a blessing sleep is when it comes! Beneficial,
sweet, and healing! Shakespeare says that sleep knits
up the raveled sleeve of care (see *Macbeth*, 2.2.37).
Sleep promises us the dawning of a new day—a new
beginning, and fresh energy and purpose to meet the
challenges of the coming day.

If we want to increase the feeling of celebration in
our lives, we should not leave all the restorative work
to sleep, however. As we open our eyes to the morning, it is a wonderful thing to create anticipation for the
hours ahead and experience the feeling of pending joy.

Much of what our day holds will be prescribed by

the obligations and circumstance of our life, but the way we feel as we rise from our bed affects the way we feel throughout the events of the day.

The Lord wants us to feel joy in the morning—and there are some ways in which we can help that to happen.

The first thing that will help us feel joy is to develop a sense of empowerment over our day. If we feel, as we rise, that the day is full of things that are required by others, then we will rise with feelings of reluctance and resistance and resentment. To feel empowered—to feel that the day is *ours*—we need to control the agenda.

"Well," you might say with real justification, "I *have* to get breakfast. I *have* to drive the children to school. I *have* to be to work on time. Or, I *have* to bathe and dress my preschoolers and be at the PTA meeting and prepare the dinner for my neighbor who has just had a baby and drive my mother to her doctor's appointment and get my husband's shirts to the laundry and . . . I have no control over what I *have* to do!!"

When you feel that way, you don't want to get out of bed. I've felt that way many a time and still do on occasion. But it is a feeling that often can be changed on almost any day, and it may not take much to do it.

We can begin by remembering that many of the responsibilities we regard as obligations put upon us by others are really just the extension of choices we made freely and eagerly on our own.

When we decided to marry, to have children, to take a certain job, we made vows, covenants, and commitments—but we made them of our own free will because we knew those decisions could be the source of joy.

When the promises and decisions we have made

turn into work or repetitive chores, we sometimes forget that we chose to make those promises, and we blame those we love for the ramifications of our role.

When we make breakfast, for example, we are not being *forced* to do that by others; we are fulfilling an aspect of the choice that we made to be a mother and a wife. We made the choice, and we are not being forced to do these things; we are doing them from a conscious and loving choice made long ago.

Understanding that, we understand that the concept of caring for those we love and have chosen to take responsibility for was part of the original vision of what we were accepting when we chose those obligations and relationships.

If we analyze most tasks that await us, we find that many are extensions of decisions we made ourselves. Suddenly we recognize that we are living the life we have chosen.

With that attitude, we can feel less trapped and more in charge of our own daily experience. We remember why and how we are doing what we do.

Other things can be done to make an "I-just-can't-wait-for-the-day-to-begin" kind of a morning.

For example, if breakfast is at the head of the chore list and you are feeling bored, tired, and resentful of the task, plan your day with a variation of breakfast. Take control of it. Here are some ideas:

• Have frozen waffles in the fridge and let the children fix their own with funny toppings.

• Go to McDonald's.

• Serve something totally outrageous, like hot fudge sundaes.

• Skip breakfast, and give everyone a breakfast bar in the car.

• Search recipe books and get up half an hour early to surprise the family with a splendid breakfast—and then let them have "do-it-yourself" breakfasts the rest of the week.

A simple change of attitude toward a burdensome task can turn it into something you anticipate rather than something you dread.

My daughter Julia, who is expecting her tenth child, makes seven school lunches every morning. It is a job she has disliked so much it was hard for her to get out of bed, because the chore of making sack lunches is the first chore she faces every day.

When I think of her making all those lunches, I remember my years of making lunches. I know just how she felt. I was always running out of bread and putting peanut butter on hamburger buns. Or else I ran out of peanut butter and had to boil eggs for egg salad (which I know not one of my children ever ate!) and by the end of the week I was scrounging for some treat to put in the sack. I'd look for something tucked in the back of the cupboard, usually those small boxes of raisins (also something my children would not eat). Some treat! I was often glad I did not have to be at school when my children opened their sacks because I knew the comments they made would be less than complimentary.

Lunches were a chore for Julia that made every morning less than joyful until the Sunday that her eight-year-old son came home from church and had the following conversation with his mother.

"What was your Primary lesson about today?" his mother asked.

"Oh, you know," young Weston said in an offhand way. "It was that story that everybody knows. You know. The one about the time Jesus was walking around the Sea of Galilee and all these thousands of people came walking after him, and they listened to him for most of the day, and then it got hot and late and they were all tired and hungry and there wasn't any food at all.

"Except, you know, for this one little boy, and his mother had remembered to pack his lunch, and so he had some loaves and fishes, and Jesus took them and fed all those people."

My daughter told me this incident, and there were tears in our eyes. "His mother had packed his lunch."

"So you see, Mother," Julia said, "I have learned to like making lunches now, because I realize that when I'm feeding my children, I am feeding the five thousand—and more. It makes me think of all the hundreds of people my children's lives will touch through the years, and I am making that possible by nourishing them as they grow up.

"Lunches are a whole new experience since I have thought of that unknown mother in Galilee who made a lunch for her little boy, and her son gave it to the Savior, and the Savior fed five thousand people with it."

That is the power of understanding the real nature of our covenants and relationships, the real nature of the chores and the humble labor we do.

Another way to feel the anticipation expressed in the phrase "I just can't wait!" is to cultivate the ability to see and celebrate the "good parts."

Good and bad are inextricably mixed together. That is the nature of mortality. The gift is to find the way to emphasize and rejoice in the good.

Sitting in the car next to a wonderful brother-in-law, I began a conversation about rearing children. He and his remarkable wife have reared a terrific family of four sons and one daughter. Their children have grown into wonderful adults, and I wanted to hear what he felt he had learned in the process.

"When I was working for a national corporation," he told me, "my company spent a great deal of money—and I spent three weeks of my time—on a course to make employees more productive. All that money and all that time were spent to teach me one thing. And it was a thing I already knew."

"What was it?" I asked eagerly.

"It's just this: if you wish to influence human behavior, the only way you can do it is by rewarding behavior that you desire to be repeated. Reward positive behavior consistently and extravagantly. All other behavior you simply ignore."

"That's it?" I exclaimed.

"The important thing," he went on, "is to know what is a true reward. It is something different for every person.

"For some, it is praise; for some, a gift; for some, companionship; for some, increased responsibility— you have to be sure it is a reward valued by the recipient and not just a standard thing which is given to everyone across the board."

To reward positive behavior, we have to train ourselves to observe and appreciate it.

How often do our children come home from school with papers or report cards and we are critical or stingy in our praise? How much more effective we would be in teaching our children to love school if we recognized in even the most faltering performance the aspects that are worthy of extravagant praise.

Without exception, praiseworthy aspects exist in

every attempt our children make. We may be so busy focusing on the things we want improved, or the disappointments, or the failures, that we neglect to pour our time, thoughts, and efforts into the portion of each attempt that is successful. The attempt itself is a measure of success.

By training ourselves to see in others and in ourselves things that are lovely, or of good report or praiseworthy—we seek the best of all that is about us, and we change the color of our own life.

Many of us become very effective at rewarding, complimenting, praising, and delighting others—but it is important that we also learn to reward ourselves as well.

If we are to feel the eagerness in our days that makes us rise with the urgency that we cannot wait for the day to begin, then we must know what we need as a reward and in some way build that feeling of reward into our own day.

We should not require others to reward us but find ways to reaffirm our worth to ourselves. If we do not, we may become martyrs, suffering imagined slights and resentments.

I have often heard women say that their lives are difficult because no one tells them how well they are doing. They say that their husbands receive praise and gratification in their work but that there are few in a woman's life to give her that kind of feedback. If our lives are to be filled with celebration, then we need to recognize our own contributions and strengths. We need to build into our lives those satisfactions that are necessary to keep us joyful.

We need to know ourselves. If we have a nature that needs adult friendship, and our husband's career is extremely demanding, and our children are young, then we should make time each day for a few minutes of the friendship that is so necessary to us to reinforce our sense of self and our feelings of joy. We need to make friends. As we begin the day, we should allow a few moments to phone a friend, meet her and her children at a park, write a letter, or reach out to someone in need.

If our personality is such that we need to feel intellectually challenged, and we find ourselves feeling deprived because we are surrounded by young children, then it is necessary for our own joy that we create moments in our day to study. There may be times when our study will have to be done at home, but some of the wonderful courses of my life have been when I have chosen a subject and studied it on my own.

My whole day takes on a special glow when I know that a book I cannot wait to read is lying in my home and that when I have my work under control, I can look forward to a few precious minutes reading and thinking. I just can't wait to get started.

Other rewards might be jogging, shopping, sewing, journal-keeping, letter-writing, painting, crafts, cooking, gardening. These are the grace notes of our lives. Moments of reward do not need to consume our life, but they need to be mixed into it, like the chocolate chips in chocolate chip cookies.

When our day dawns and we open our eyes to face the list of things to be done, if we feel the list consists of things we have chosen and decided—if we change our attitude about the tasks before us—if we look for what is good, sweet, and of worth in our life and in those around us, and, finally, if we have crafted our day so that there are moments and experiences of personal reward to look forward to, then we will find ourselves greeting the morning with joy.

In celebration, we will sit up in bed and say, "I just can't wait!"

Beauty is truth, truth beauty,—that is all
Ye know on earth, and all ye need to know.

John Keats, 1795–1821

9

....

The "Ode on a
Grecian Urn" Mentality

$\mathcal{M}$y father was a rancher. He was a rancher
by profession. He was a rancher by education. He was
a rancher as an investor. And he was a rancher out of
love. My father loved the glory and the beauty of the
untried land and the limitless possibilities of the West.
And as an agricultural scientist, my father believed he
could harvest those possibilities and teach others to
use them wisely, productively, and well. My mother
always said, caught somewhere between admiration
and exasperation, "Charles never saw a piece of land
he didn't want to own." My mother was a woman of
the city—she did not like ranch life.

We lived in the city. Father's ranches were run by
ranch managers. Father's business offices were in the
city, and he was bishop of our ward for many years, so
free time—a rarity—almost always entailed a quick
drive out to one of the ranches.

Those drives are some of the most precious memories of my childhood. We would speed along the

stretch of seemingly endless road that led straight to the horizon where the Rocky Mountains stood like a smoky blue ruffle between the land and the great, turquoise bowl of the prairie sky. On either side of us the vast acreage of Alberta spread like a quilt that had just been shaken and was settling down onto its vast bed. The fallow fields of strip farming rolled like ribbons across the incomprehensible space. The huge fields of mustard, more golden than the buttercups, the seas of blue flax blowing in the constant breeze, and the oceans of wheat waving their heavy, grain-laden heads stretched on forever.

Sometimes my father, in his passion for the miracle of the productive land, would pull the car to the side of the narrow, dusty road. He'd walk down the barrow pit that separated the road from the fields and snap off a few heads of wheat. "I've never seen such full heads!" he would exclaim. "That's Ed Sorenson's field. I'll need to ask him what seed he used, when he planted, and how he prepared the soil. This will be a record-breaking yield!"

He knew the name of every tree, shrub, and wildflower—not just the common name but the Latin name and the botanical family. When we traveled as a family, he kept a record of any trees or plants he did not recognize, and when we got home (if he could not learn the answer by asking people on the way) he researched until he identified each one.

On every drive, at least once, my father would talk about the land. "Have you ever seen anything more beautiful?" he would ask. He would stop the car and wave his hand at the vista as though it were a great pageant and he was the impresario.

A brilliant sunset would bring him to silence. The

car would roll to a halt, and my father would gaze at the dying sun staining the air with the colors of peonies and hollyhocks and nightshade—and he would stand transfixed by the beauty. The silhouette of a threshing machine, black against the vivid sky, the chaff spewing like a plume against the crimson and orange streaks, added mystery and motion.

He savored such moments as he would a symphony, and his reverence of that glory was transmitted to his children. We could not have felt closer to the Lord than we did in the fields and the mountains.

When my father died of a heart attack at a too-young age, he had not had time to secure his estate. All of his older children were in graduate schools in the States, and our mother was left with two teenagers plus three ranches and a herd of registered Herefords that she had neither the training, the interest, nor the emotional wherewithal to manage.

Years later, as I was driving home to New York with six of my children, my fourteen-year-old nephew, John, sat next to me in the front seat. I told John how his father, my brother Malcolm, had worked each summer on the ranches. In the midst of one of my stories, John looked at me earnestly. In his face was all the curiosity and intensity of a child who has seen the gleam of the past and wants to know exactly the truth of it all.

"Aunt Jerry," he said, peering at me with his intelligent, demanding eyes, "how come, if our family owned so much of Alberta, how come we don't own so much as an acre now? How come?"

How come, indeed! It was hard for me to think that all the things that I and my siblings had taken for granted as children were gone, slipped through tired, grieving, inattentive fingers, lost to dishonest, manipulative businessmen, sold for educations and new houses and lost forever to a family that now never really returned to Canada except to visit.

Mother, and Mother alone, remained in the Canadian city of our childhood. Through the years we children made pilgrimages to see her, and perhaps in our hearts all of us wondered, "What if the ranches were still ours? Where *did* the lost lands of our youth go?" We were a family that did not discuss such things.

This year my mother's dear heart, which had loved us with unswerving care through her ninety-two years, stopped beating, quietly, in her sleep. Our mother, who had taught us to love words, literature, music, art, flowers, friends, generosity, and one another; our mother, who had given us the gift of beauty as though it fell, by nature, from her hands; our dear mother was gone, and the family gathered. At last her long, long widowhood was over, and we felt in our own sadness her great rejoicing at being reunited with her beloved Charles.

It was a poignant farewell for all of us. We said good-bye to our mother in mortality, knowing we would see her again, but still, in this lifetime we were motherless. Such a strange, unprotected feeling, even in our mature years. We knew, however, that we were not just saying farewell to our beloved mother. We were also saying farewell to Canada, the land of our childhood. Nothing was left to draw us back to this land of our childhood again. It was a weight in our minds and hearts.

As I drove northward toward Calgary to catch my late evening plane home to California, the prolonged twilight of Canadian summer lay across the land like a blessing. That soft prairie twilight has a most unusual light—as sweet and clear as a hymn. Suddenly, as we drove down the coulee, across a familiar bridge on the Oldman River, and then up a curving turn onto the flat, golden prairies once more, I said to my brother, "Stop the car!"

There, spread before us, were the fields of flax and mustard, the sky stained with sunset, the glint of the faraway river, the smoky outline of the Rockies, and the endless horizon of our youth. We had seen it a hundred times. From this very spot. And here it was, just as it had been in our childhood when our father taught us to see and love it.

At that moment we were seeing this land in reality, but I suddenly realized these vistas, this wondrous presence of the land of my birth was always with me—in my heart, in my mind, and in my memory.

This land belonged to us, to my brothers and sister, just as the air, and the sun, and the great visual celebration of the magnificence of this earth belongs to all of us. We have only to open our heart to see it and to love it.

The earth is the Lord's and the fulness thereof, and he has given it to us for our joy, our memory, our teaching, to learn the truth of beauty and the beauty of truth.

My inheritance is real, untouchable, eternal—it is more real, lasting, and precious than the land itself. Alberta is ours in our hearts, in our ability to appreciate, remember, and express its beauty.

Our father and mother have given us the most lasting, endless, and profound inheritance that it is possible to give: they have given us the eyes, the heart, and the mind to see and appreciate beauty. They gave us the memories that cannot fade and that open up the understanding of loveliness that makes all things more precious. There are no lost acres in Alberta. I carry them with me in my heart. My father gave them to me at the roadside when I was a little girl as he waved his hand so that I would see.

The gift of daily celebration is bound up in our ability to see the hand of the Lord, the Creator, in all things—to see beauty in every manifestation of creation, in the talents of others as they are inspired by God, and in others themselves, because they, too, are creations of the Lord.

The appreciation of beauty is like all other talents. It increases when we study, practice, and labor to develop it. We can read books about art, nature, and music. We can attend art museums, listen to fine music, and read exquisite literature. We can walk in nature and look for both the large vistas and the small, lovely things.

We can train ourselves to see beauty and grace in everyone whose path crosses ours.

A wonderful short story by Philip Roth called "Pigeon Feathers" tells the thoughts of a teenage boy who questions if there could be any sense to the universe, whether there is any purpose, any God.

Angry and rebellious, he goes out to the barn and shoots some pigeons who have been stealing the chicken feed. Suddenly he is sickened by what he is doing, and he picks up the body of one of the birds. As he does so, he stares at the feathers, each feather so perfect, so delicately colored, so precisely fashioned, so finely wrought in every detail.

He feels a weight lift from his spirit. If God could

take infinite care to create such beauty in a single feather of a single pigeon, then surely he must know and care about the heart of a boy.

Beauty is the celebration of our lives. It gives us comfort, hope, delight, motivation, and the knowledge that we are loved. It is our noble inheritance from the Lord.

Love is, above all, the gift of oneself.

Jean Anouilh, 1910–

10

....

The As-You-Wish Heart

$\mathcal{I}$n William Golding's *The Princess Bride*, Wesley, the poor farm boy, complies with the heroine's demands by saying, "As you wish." Finally she realizes that "as you wish" is his way of saying, "I love you." What a perfect translation!

Nothing creates a life of celebration more than the ability to love, to live in an atmosphere of our own loving feelings for others and of our desire to show that love. Love requires nothing of others. It is not a coin with which we barter. Love rejoices in service. Love sees with tender eyes. Love forgives and forgets. Love does not judge. Love searches for ways to grace and bless the lives of others. Love knows no barriers. Love builds bridges. Love has courage and does not fail. Love is its own reward.

None of us loves perfectly, but if we are to take upon ourselves the countenance of Christ, then it should be our goal to become more and more perfect in the love which we feel and in our means of expressing it. We are told that God is love.

Love heals wounds. Love shines brightness into

dark corners. Love lifts selfish concerns. Love teaches us how to rejoice.

Love lets us see with another's eyes.

I was to meet my teenage son at the door of the school to drive him home. After waiting for a long time, I drove around the school to the back door. Not there either. There were no students left at the school, so I assumed he had gotten another ride home.

It was a bitterly cold Connecticut day, and I had left the other children at home engaged in homework—with supper preparations half begun. Annoyed, and a little worried, I drove home. He was not there. I returned to the school. Waited. Drove around to the other doors and went home a second time.

Still no William. Very worried, I sped back to the school, frantically thinking what to do next. As I drove down the road I saw our other car, with my oldest son driving, and William beside him. I honked, and William came over and climbed into my car. My other son continued home.

Totally out of control with relief, frustration, anger, and puzzlement, I began lecturing my William without giving him a chance to say a word.

I went on for ten minutes about how, when I made arrangements to meet him, I expected him to be there. I told him how much he had worried me. I expressed how desperately worried I had been, how totally inconsiderate his actions were, and how frustrating it had been to sit waiting at the door, to drive around looking for him, to drive home, to put all of my work on hold, and on and on.

Finally I calmed down enough to really look at his face. His cheeks were red with cold and, to my horror, I saw tears standing in his eyes.

"Oh, William," I exclaimed, "I'm not mad at you. It's just that I have been so worried and frustrated. I've been waiting for you for *two hours!*"

There was a moment of absolute silence, and then William said quietly, "I've been waiting for two hours, too, Mother."

Never has the message of loving come more swiftly or sharply to my heart. All I could see in my self-involvement—in my own emotions, my own inconvenience, and my own disrupted day—was how hard my day had been. In one quiet sentence my son taught me that the eyes of love would have looked to see what his day had been.

It turned out that he had been waiting the whole time outdoors in the cold for fear of missing me. He had waited at the back door, and then, after waiting for extended periods, would go to look at the other door. For two hours we had played round-robin around the school, apparently just missing one another.

The first lesson of the as-you-wish heart is that it sees the wishes and needs of others swiftly, carefully, and compassionately, and serves those needs to the best of its ability. We should train our heart to feel not what we want, not what we had hoped, but rather what the loved one is feeling and how we can help. We should see the situation from the other person's focus, not from our own.

My husband always answers the phone, "How can I help you?" In another person that might seem a meaningless social phrase, but when my husband says it, it is a promise.

One lesson I learned from the scriptures that is helpful to me in training my thoughts, my heart, and my spirit in feeling refreshed and tender love toward my children comes from the prophet Mormon. When he writes to his son, Moroni, or addresses him directly, he says, "Moroni, my beloved son . . . "

I have found that as I speak to my husband and my children, if I allow that phrase to run through my mind, my heart is instantly warmed. As I say the name I add (either silently or out loud) "my beloved child," "my beloved husband," "my beloved friend."

When I meet someone I find hard to feel genuine affection for, I try to imagine what he or she was like as a little child. Since I have never met a child I didn't like, this method works for me.

Sometimes I can see a proud and difficult man as a serious, lonely child. Sometimes I can see a cold and controlling woman as an intense and determined child afraid that if she did not always do her best something terrible would happen. Seeing the seeds of adult behavior helps make me more compassionate and to believe in the basic goodness of even the most difficult people.

When stress and pressure arise in my relationship with my husband, my technique reminds me of the river of love which is the mainstream of my existence. Sometimes that love becomes obscured in the moment, and, before I let myself say or do anything, I look at my husband and say in my mind, "This is the dearest person in the entire world to me. He is the kindest, most wonderful man I have ever known. I love him with all my heart." The moment it takes to think these thoughts makes all the difference. I think those thoughts every time I see him and it is a joyous and comforting reaffirmation.

The love of brothers and sister, nieces and nephews, in-laws, grandchildren, friends, neighbors, business associates, and even strangers is the explosion of celebration in the life of one who has learned how to live with love.

Here is a bouquet of ideas for celebrating love in your life:

Letter Writing

Keep on hand in your home a supply of unusual stationery, colored pens, a beautiful fountain pen, a roll of stamps, greeting cards, pretty stickers, rubber stamp and pad—and other things to make a note seem special and fun to write. How often have you thought of a line you want to drop to someone, and because you do not have a nice card on hand or the stamps, you neglect writing the note until it would no longer be timely. What a missed opportunity!

Write thank-you notes for everything—to a speaker who gave a good talk in sacrament meeting, to the Primary president when you have seen some wonderful evidence of the great work being done in Primary, to a teenager who has done something fine, to a faraway friend whose name just pops into your mind. Learn to look for chances to feel and express gratitude.

If you see a newspaper clipping about a friend, or if you read a magazine article that you think your friend would like, clip it and send it. What a nice way to say "thinking of you."

Decorate envelopes and notes. One of my grandchildren sent me a letter, and at the bottom he wrote, "When you answer my letter, please answer it fancy." I often draw little cartoons of my grandchildren and me at the bottom of their letters depicting a pretend conversation written in balloons coming out of our mouths. It is their favorite kind of "fancy."

Keep your special stationery, cards, stamps, and

such in a place that the rest of the family cannot raid, and then you will always be able to respond to your impulse to write a letter. It only takes a moment to do it, but often the effect of a graceful letter will last a lifetime.

Love at Home

Have a supply of things in your home that will give you the opportunity to express love. We each have different resources depending on our interests, our financial and time constraints, and so on, but we can all have something we can use to express our love—if only a telephone.

Flowers are a wonderful way to express love. If you love gardening, be sure that some of what you grow will be things that can be shared. Try roses, pansies, tomatoes, zucchini (even better when made into bread), clusters of fresh herbs—whatever you find easy to grow.

Crafts and sewing are very satisfying talents to share. The spectrum is as wide as the interests of those who work with their hands. One young woman discovered a great-looking—and easy—pattern for a summer maternity dress. She knew another woman who was expecting a baby the same time as she was, and so, when she bought fabric, she bought a second length of a different fabric, and then carrying machine, fabric, and pattern, she went to visit her sister—and they spent the afternoon watching their children play and sewing two adorable dresses. That is the loving heart thinking as-you-wish.

Books and magazines can be a great outlet for love. When we read a book that gives us delight, it is a great act of loving celebration to share that book. I know of women who, as soon as they read a book, write in the front of it their name, the date they finished the book, and what they thought about it. Then they give the book to a friend and encourage her to do the same and then pass the book along. Such books become treasures both of literature and of love.

Games and music are other evidences of love in a home—and of the opportunity to show love to others. We have a nephew, who, when he visits, always comes with the latest game. We have the most glorious evenings with him!

Music is such a joy to share. I love to teach visiting children new songs, especially at Thanksgiving and Christmas. I love to discover new songs, new music, and share it with others, knowing how it will bless their lives. The most cherished books in my music library are books I have been introduced to by dear friends.

One Christmas we invited family and friends over, asking each family to bring a new and unusual Christmas song to teach to the group. We sang away in a room filled with love, and then, after eating, we walked in the dark to the top of a hill that overlooked the town of San Juan Capistrano, twinkling with lights in the velvet night. Children and adults stood and sang to the stars. It was a wonderful night of love.

In our homes we should always have a room or a place where a guest would be instantly welcome. Even if it is only a couch, the blankets and clean sheets should be at hand. Then, when love urges us to invite, we can do so without hesitation.

The humblest guest room can be filled with love with a thoughtfully chosen book, a fresh water glass, flowers or candy on the bedside table, and genuine joy and welcome in the heart of the hosts.

Food: The Gift of Love

Develop some food item that is easy for you to make or keep on hand, and keep on hand a supply of it or the ingredients to make it. For example:

• Frozen or cooked jam.

• Breads of every kind.

• Applesauce.

• Soup—my particular favorite because I have so many good soup recipes: chili soup (always a hit); German meatball soup; corn chowder; hamburger vegetable soup, etc.

• Pies, cookies, and cakes—especially in today's world, homemade sweets have become a wonderful treat.

When I take food to someone, I take it in a disposable or nonreturnable container because returning dishes is a real pain. It's always nice to add a ribbon, or a flower, or a pretty dishcloth, or bright wrapping. Little touches make a celebration.

Sometimes just pizza and root beer show love best of all. Pizza says, "I don't have time to cook—we're in this boat together—but I want you to know I care." Sometimes such candor is a gift in and of itself.

Service

Service is really a privilege. It is very difficult for others to let us into their lives to actually care for them and their needs. We should treat such opportunities with the respect they deserve.

Sometimes the best service is to listen with love and concern.

Sometimes we serve by allowing others to serve us—which is, in many ways, one of the hardest forms of service of all.

Search for meaningful ways to serve, and be sure to

apply the "as-you-wish" rule. We don't serve to make ourselves feel better but to look for what the real needs are and then serve those needs.

Find splendid ways to rejoice when others rejoice. Balloons, confetti, flowers, cookie bouquets, a red carpet, an unexpected treat—when a missionary comes home, when someone gets a promotion, when a baby is born or a child has graduated.

I once heard a child talking to an older relative at the airport as they were waiting for their returned missionary to step off the plane. "We have balloons all over the house!" the child exclaimed, her voice trembling with the thrill of it. "We have . . . oh . . . I don't know . . . probably more than three hundred balloons—just thousands and thousands of them!"

Parties, Hospitality, and Entertainment

The giving of parties can be a true celebration of love. Here are some of our parties that have grown from love:

• A three-day house party, with our brothers and sisters and their spouses all sleeping under one roof. Each day was crammed with everything we love—walks on the beach, talks on family history, news of our children, visits to museums, meals at restaurants, singing around the piano, a visit to the San Diego Temple. The high point of the party was a dinner in which we went to a farmers market and everyone bought the makings for one dish of their own choosing. Each couple prepared their contribution to the meal. It was the most delicious meal ever—and we had such great fun crowded in the kitchen working around one another, preparing surprises—fresh fruit salad, tossed salad, special rolls, spaghetti, fried chicken, and a scrumptious berry pie.

• A Christmas party, to which we invite a mix of guests—family, neighbors, friends, and ward members. We have a light buffet supper and then we sit in a circle and everyone recounts a precious Christmas memory. It sounds so simple, but some of the dearest moments of my life have been as friends or neighbors have shared something so tender and unexpected that we have seen into their heart.

• A party for a visitor with a special interest or talent. We have an evening of learning or entertainment, and we are edified and entertained among friends. Travel reports, musical talents, scriptural discussions— those listening are blessed, and those who have an opportunity to share things dear to their heart feel loved and appreciated.

• Our Advent calendar party, given the first week of December. We invite families with all their children for an informal supper, and then we scatter throughout the house to work at different tables and on different work spaces to make advent calendars from construction paper, Christmas stickers, old Christmas cards, and so on. It is great family fun!

My favorite calendar party was topped off by a group of teenage boys starting to sing "O Christmas Tree." They got through the first line, "O Christmas tree, O Christmas tree," and then they began to ad lib, still singing the tune, "Nobody knows the words to this song, And no one can sing it, except the guy who wrote it, and he is probably dead by now— O Christmas tree, O Christmas tree . . . "

Verbal Expressions of Love

Just say it. When you see someone looking lovely— say it. When someone has done a good job—say it.

When you think a good thought—say it. When you recognize the hand of the Lord—say it.

Words of kindness and love could seed our lives with a harvest of celebration if we could just train ourselves to feel and say them.

Gratitude is the food of love—and it is the fruit of love as well. We should not only express our love but learn to live with grateful hearts. Appreciation and gratitude erase bitterness and disappointment.

Forgiveness is also an essential ingredient of celebration. If we carry past wrongs chained to our minds and spirits, we, like Marley's ghost, cannot be free or happy.

We have not truly forgiven until we truly forget. Just let it go. Do not yearn for justice, or suspend yourself on the dry-dock of "it's not fair"; do not nurse hard feelings and hurts and think that somehow in your suffering you punish the other. Believe that the Lord will make everything right and fair when we all come to the bar. I, for one, am hoping for mercy, and so I pray and struggle to give it to those who have injured me or my loved ones. When the Lord told us to love our enemies, he meant that we must find it in our hearts to love them. Perfect love casteth out fear and hate and envy and pain.

The real danger in being unforgiving is not so much that we fail to forgive our enemies as that we often fail to forgive our loved ones. We nurse hurts and slights from our parents, our spouses, and our children. We remember past wrongs and mistakes, and we will not let our love go past them. In moments of stress we dredge them up to hurt and punish and limit those whom we have promised to cherish.

In every relationship are acts, both intended and

unintended, that hurt the other. If we are to live with joy and celebration, we must work those through, resolve them, forgive, and *forget* them. True love lets others grow beyond the past—and remembers it no more.

Unexpected Gestures of Love

We lived in a ward with a child of six who seemed like love embodied. She was interested in everyone. She knew the names of the people in the ward—of every age. When she entered the building, her feet seemed to dance with eagerness. Her lovely little face was bright with joyful expectation, intelligence, and delight at everything she saw and heard. One Fast Sunday she walked up to the pulpit. Her feet were a little hesitant, and we could see she felt a little shy and overwhelmed by the long walk up the aisle, but she knew she wanted to bear her testimony. With a deep breath for courage, she stepped up onto the children's step and stood by the microphone. Her face was shining with its usual smile and she looked out at the congregation with such open-hearted joy and affection that we all felt our hearts leap out to her. After she had said the usual words of a child's testimony, she stood for another moment smiling at us. "I love everyone in this ward," she said. Her six-year-old voice was clear and strong. "I think of you every night, and I remember you in my prayers. I always pray that all of you will have sweet dreams—that nothing will trouble you."

As long as we lived in that ward I felt the influence of that child's loving prayer upon my dreams. What a perfect expression of love. That is the talent of a loving heart—to give unexpected, perfect gifts.

In that same ward I received another remarkable gift of love.

I had been hit by a car as I was jogging and spent a year in difficult recovery. During that time I was called to be the ward music director. I loved the calling, and though I could stand only with the help of a walker—and eventually, a cane—for most of that year, still I rejoiced in teaching and singing the hymns of the Lord.

One Sunday I challenged the ward to memorize the hymns in the new hymnbook. "We have memorized the hymns of our childhood because we have been singing them for so many years," I said, "but now, we do not have all of those years left to us—and there are so many beautiful new hymns. We must memorize them consciously—just like the Primary children memorize all those wonderful songs every year for their Sunday Primary program."

Then I showed the congregation how easily they could memorize the hymn "How Great Thou Art" by having them sing the first verse without their hymnbooks.

The next three weeks I was away from the city, so I turned my music responsibilities over to my dear friend Joyce Jacobson, who serves the Lord with a heart of pure love. When I returned, I stood to begin the music practice.

As soon as I stood up, the organist began to play "How Great Thou Art." I signaled her that it was the wrong hymn, but she merely smiled and went on playing. The entire congregation stood, and then I noticed no one was holding a hymnbook. By memory the congregation began to sing that mighty hymn.

Tears sprang to my eyes. I stood transfixed as I looked at their beloved faces and listened to the words of that glorious hymn. They sang the first verse, then the second, then the third, and finally the fourth. All memorized. From youngest children to the oldest members, from families to singles, every member of that congregation sang with one heart, with one voice. Never has music sounded more sweetly or faces been more beautiful.

Joyce, I was told later, had passed out the words, and the slips had been placed on sinks and dashboards and dinner tables. The whole ward had united in love to create a moment of perfect love. I know the angels sang with them, too. In that chapel, that morning, I believe I experienced that emotion which is called "the perfect love of Christ." They who sang had received his image in their countenances.

Such unexpected, perfect moments are the gift the Lord gives when our true hearts' desire is to feel and express love. In that process of living by love, our hearts become, miraculously, as-we-wish.

Joy is the purpose for which we were made and framed by our Heavenly Father. As Shakespeare said, "What a piece of work [we are]! How noble in reason! How infinite in faculty! In form and moving how express and admirable! In action how like an angel! In apprehension how like a god! The beauty of the world!" (*Hamlet*, 2.2. 315–18). It is in love that we find ourselves, and everything that has meaning and worth.

Years ago I attended a performance of *Pippin* on the New York stage. In the play the stagemaster tries to influence Pippin, the son of the powerful emperor Charlemagne. The young Pippin is full of ambition and immaturity, and the guileful stagemaster urges the young man to give his life meaning. First he urges

Pippin to seek power. When that doesn't work to give meaning to Pippin's life, he convinces Pippin to seek fame and then to seek the pleasures of the world. When all has failed, Pippin, heartsick and weary, stumbles onto a farm, and there meets a sweet widow and her little son.

Pippin becomes a farmer, marries the widow, and becomes a father to the young boy.

The stagemaster is furious. He ridicules Pippin, and castigates him, and berates him. "How can you trade all the glamour and power and achievement of the world for this paltry farm, for this ordinary woman? If you listen to me, you can have every wonderful thing the world has to offer."

Pippin refuses to listen to the enticements of the stagemaster. He and his wife and child stand in the center of the stage, holding hands, and they begin to sing.

The stagemaster, driven to rage, shouts, "Well, let's see how well you can sing when I take away the farm," and the farm disappears from the stage. Pippin and his wife and child keep singing. Then, one by one, the stagemaster takes away the scenery, the huge lights, the backdrop, even their outer clothes. Finally the orchestra even ceases playing, until only one last note of the piano is heard, and then silence.

Pippin stands on a bare stage, with nothing but the brick wall and stage ropes behind him. He is dressed in a homespun shirt and trousers. Just one bare little bulb hangs in the center of the stage. Silence is all around. Everything has been taken away.

"Now," the stagemaster says, "now see if you can sing."

Pippin holds his wife's hand tighter. Their little boy

steps close to his mother and father, and the three of them stand, in their simple homespun clothes. Softly their song begins.

Their voices grow stronger and stronger, and the theater is filled with the sound of joy. Love seems to shimmer in the air, and the stage, bare as it is, is the most beautiful stage I have ever seen. Nothing but a man, a woman, a child—and love. Paul said in his tender epistle to the Ephesians:

"That Christ may dwell in your hearts by faith; that ye, being rooted and ground in love, may be able to comprehend with all saints what is the breadth, and length, and depth, and height; and to know the love of Christ, which passeth knowledge, that ye might be filled with all the fulness of God . . . abundantly above all that we ask or think" (Ephesians 3:17–20).

Celebration!

Index

145

INDEX